The Morning Meeting Book

Karen Poplawski

FOURTH EDITION

Responsive Classroom®

First edition published 1999. Fourth edition 2023.

ISBN: 978-1-950317-46-2
Library of Congress Control Number: 2023937916

Principal Photography by Jeff Woodward. Videography by Tom Adams

Center for Responsive Schools, Inc.
85 Avenue A, P.O. Box 718
Turners Falls, MA 01376-0718

800-360-6332
www.responsiveclassroom.org

Contents

Foreword

"It Mattered That I Came"

In the spring of my first year as a secondary school teacher, I got a letter from a student for whom I had a particular fondness, letting me know that she was dropping out of school. School wasn't making much sense to her, and little that she was being asked to learn held much interest for her. She wrote, almost apologetically, that school just wasn't a place where she felt she belonged. More than twenty years later, her words still seem profoundly sad to me:

> I will always remember how you said, "Hi, Sue," as I walked into eighth period. It made me feel like it really mattered that I came.

It touched and pained me that something that seemed so small to me, an act I hadn't even been aware of, had meant so much to her. I vowed to learn something from it and became more intentional about greeting students. I stationed myself by the door and tried to say a little something to each one as they entered, or at least to make eye contact and smile at every student, not just the ones like Sue for whom I had an instinctive affinity.

Gradually, I realized how much I was learning at my post by the door. I observed who bounced in with head up and smile wide, whose eyes were red-rimmed from tears shed in the girls' room at lunch, who mumbled a response into their collar and averted their eyes every day for an entire semester. I didn't know what to do about much of it, but at least I was learning how to notice.

I have learned a lot since then. It is important for students to be noticed, to be seen by their teacher. But it is only a start; it is not enough by itself. Students must notice and be noticed by each other as well.

Years after I taught Sue, I joined the staff of Greenfield Center School, the independent K–8 school founded by Northeast Foundation for Children (the former name of Center for Responsive Schools). There, I saw teachers teaching students to greet each other, to speak to each other, to listen to each other. I saw students start each day together in Morning Meeting, where noticing and being noticed were explicit goals.

This book is about Morning Meeting—a particular and deliberate way to begin the school day. Today, many students in elementary schools around the country launch their school days with Morning Meeting.

In Morning Meeting, all classroom members—grown-ups and students—gather in a circle, greet each other, and listen and respond to each other's news. We take note of who is present and who is absent, whether it is still raining or not, who is smiling and buoyant, who is having a hard time smiling. We practice academic skills, briefly grapple with problems that challenge our minds, and look forward to the learning we'll do together in the day ahead. Morning Meeting allows us to begin each day as a community of caring and respectful learners.

—Roxann Kriete

These words, written by the original author of *The Morning Meeting Book*, carry an almost prophetic tone as we revisit this vignette in a postpandemic educational landscape. Now more than ever, we understand the importance of being seen, being heard, and knowing that it matters we came to school. Although Roxann couldn't possibly know how powerful the book's contents would be when she first penned it over two decades ago, hundreds of thousands of educators and millions of students worldwide have since benefited from the power of the Morning Meeting.

The practice of *Responsive Classroom* Morning Meeting grew out of the work of a group of educators at the Greenfield Center School that Roxann references. This simple yet profound practice accomplishes so much in such a short time. It is a timeless gift to the field of education. With this new edition, we pay homage to the educators who established this practice. They were simply trying to make the lives of the students they served better and build a more positive learning environment, a place where every student belonged, felt significant, and experienced joy. As we bring you the fourth edition of this well-loved manuscript, we aim to both maintain and build upon the legacy of these founding educators.

—Karen Poplawski for *Responsive Classroom*

New in This Edition

We took great care in both preserving time-honored content from the previous editions of *The Morning Meeting Book* and curating new content to meet the needs of its current readers and users. The following is an overview of some of the updates and changes you will find:

- **User-Friendly Design:** This new edition has a full-color interior with photographs, icons, charts, and color-coding to help readers easily navigate the different components and concepts within this book.

- **Updated Content:** We curated new ideas for each component and expanded implementation guidance. We also included a new chapter devoted to harnessing the power of the Morning Meeting structure to build community and foster connections outside the classroom setting.

- **Digital Tools:** Videos of Morning Meeting in action, along with digital tools for planning meaningful Morning Meetings, can now be found on responsiveclassroom.org and via QR code in this book.

Introduction

A group of students entered the office doors well past the bell that indicated it was time to sign in. Their bus was late again. The students lamented to the assistant principal and principal:

> "We're late all the time!"
> "We probably missed Morning Meeting again!"
> "It isn't fair that we don't get to do Morning Meeting!"

As they voiced their disgruntlement, the superintendent of the school district, Dr. Johnson, happened to show up for one of his regular visits to the school. The students turned to Dr. Johnson and said, "You're the boss. Can't you do something about these buses so we don't keep missing Morning Meeting?"

Dr. Johnson, curious, asked the students why it was so important they be in Morning Meeting. They readily supplied him with a list of reasons.

"We get to learn about each other!"

"We get to learn names and play games together."

"It just helps us start our day off right."

"It's our favorite part of the day, and we missed it again!"

Their passionate pleas did not fall on deaf ears. Dr. Johnson immediately worked with the director of transportation to ensure their bus arrived on time so these students could fully participate in Morning Meeting every day.

These students are among millions of students who look forward to starting each day with Morning Meeting. This phenomenon is due in part to the intuitive nature of the design of the Morning Meeting. Driven by the work of psychologists and educational theorists including Maslow, Dreikurs, and Adler, Morning Meeting is designed to meet a human's basic and instinctive need and desire for social stability, interpersonal relationships, affiliation, and connectedness. In the opening vignette, the students' motivation to seek help and ensure they could participate in Morning Meeting was, at its core, a fight for their right to belong, be seen, feel significant, and feel connected to those with whom they share their day.

Cultivating Connections

We are social beings, and our need to connect is instinctive. At a time when having a "strong connection" more likely refers to having a Wi-Fi signal rather than a meaningful relationship with someone, intentionally cultivating those face-to-face connections is even more important.

The research is clear regarding the power and importance of human connection, and specifically face-to-face connections. The single best predictor of healthy emotional interactions is a lot of face-to-face communication, which is also the best way to learn emotions and develop human-contact skills (Rideout et al. 2010). But the amount of time that students experience face-to-face interaction and connectedness is diminishing as it competes with an increase in screen time. Seventy-five percent of two-year-olds and 67 percent of two-to-five-year-olds spend more time in front of the screen than is recommended. Children ranging from birth to eight years old have an average of 2.5 hours per day of screen time. Screen time then increases significantly, with children between eight and ten years old spending six hours a day in front of the screen (Susic 2023).

Additionally, the source for learning and nurturing basic needs for connection has changed as parent and family relationships have shifted. A recent survey calculated that Americans are enjoying just thirty-seven minutes of "quality time" as a family on weekdays (Renner 2018). Another survey conducted with one thousand British parents found that the average parent spends a mere five hours per week communicating face-to-face with their children (Renner 2020). With the hustle and bustle of every day lives, finding time to pause, sit and connect with others can be challenging for families. Put simply, students may not have a lot of practice with the types of face to face communication that is vital for healthy social and emotional development.

This information significantly impact educators, who need to create spaces where students can cultivate meaningful human connections and provide students with opportunities to practice building relationships and connecting with others in a face-to-face environment. It is these types of meaningful interactions that allow students to consistently feel safe, have fun, and enjoy a sense of significance and belonging—basic human needs that are becoming increasingly rare for today's students.

Think back to the story that opened this chapter and the passion those students felt as they advocated for their collective needs for fun, significance, and belonging. Every student deserves to begin their day with a Morning Meeting where they are an important voice within a caring, respectful community. Morning Meeting should be the cornerstone of every student's day in every school, and educators should support it as wholeheartedly as Dr. Johnson did. Morning Meeting is a microcosm of the way we wish our schools to be—communities full of learning, safe and respectful and challenging for all. Daily Morning Meeting builds the foundation for positive communities in and out of school, learning that students will carry with them for the rest of their lives.

The *Responsive Classroom* Approach

The Morning Meeting format described in this book was developed by Northeast Foundation for Children, now Center for Responsive Schools, and is a key practice of the *Responsive Classroom* approach.

The *Responsive Classroom* approach is a student-centered social and emotional learning approach to teaching and discipline. It is comprised of a set of research- and evidence-based practices designed to create safe, joyful, and engaging classroom and school communities for both students and teachers. Schools and teachers adopting the *Responsive Classroom* approach focus on:

- Creating optimal learning conditions for students to develop the academic, social, and emotional skills needed for success in and out of school

- Building positive school and classroom communities where students learn, behave, hope, and set and achieve goals

The core belief of the *Responsive Classroom* approach is that, in order to be successful in and out of school, students need to learn a set of social and emotional competencies—cooperation, assertiveness, responsibility, empathy, and self-control—and a set of academic competencies—academic mindset, perseverance, learning strategies, and academic behaviors.

The *Responsive Classroom* approach is informed by the work of educational theorists and the experiences of exemplary classroom teachers. Six principles guide this approach:

- Teaching social and emotional skills is as important as teaching academic content.

- How we teach is as important as what we teach.

- Great cognitive growth occurs through social interaction.

- How we work together as adults to create a safe, joyful, and inclusive school environment is as important as our individual contribution or competence.

- What we know and believe about our students—individually, culturally, developmentally—informs our expectations, reactions, and attitudes about those students.

- Partnering with families—knowing them and valuing their contributions—is as important as knowing the children we teach.

Visit www.responsiveclassroom.org to learn more about the array of practices that work in tandem with Morning Meeting to create safe, joyful, and engaging classrooms and schools.

How to Use This Book

You may choose to read the entire book from beginning to end, select sections that immediately grab your attention, or use the book as a reference as your Morning Meeting experience grows. The book begins with an overview chapter about Morning Meeting as a whole. Next come chapters about each of the four Morning Meeting components. The final chapter highlights ways to harness the power of the Morning Meeting format to create a sense of belonging within the schoolwide community.

Each chapter follows a predictable structure to guide readers to a deeper understanding of Morning Meeting and to help readers navigate the book easily. Each chapter includes the following sections:

- **Classroom Vignette**—Each chapter begins with a section that illustrates aspects of Morning Meeting in action. These glimpes take you into the middle of classrooms where Morning Meetings are flourishing. Some of these vignettes are from large urban schools; some are from small rural schools. While the settings for the vignettes vary, one thing remains consistent—they provide relatable exemplars of the power and impact of Morning Meeting.

- **Overview**—In this section, we briefly define the focus of the chapter and outline key aspects of the highlighted component. These descriptions are intended to provide, in very simple terms, a foundational understanding of what each component entails.

- **Purposes**—This section articulates the purposes and goals of each component and how it fits into the larger context of learning. It highlights and interprets some of the powerful moments created in classrooms and conveys some of the specific details and flavor of well-run Morning Meetings.

- **Getting Started**—In this section, you'll find recommendations to help you as you begin to implement the components of Morning Meeting. The suggestions and examples are offered as templates to be used for guidance, not as exact patterns for repetition. Your knowledge of each class's development, pace, and needs— and of your own teaching style—will lead to adaptations that work best for you and the students you teach. These recommendations are offered with respect for individual teachers and a wish to empower them. They are also offered with the awareness, affirmed by thousands of teachers with whom we have worked, that templates drawn by experienced hands are invaluable tools when starting to do something new. Feel free to use these templates—trace them, adapt them, refine them so that they truly serve you. Just keep the purposes and goals of Morning Meeting in mind as you go. Each Getting Started section ends with a concise listing of teacher and student responsibilities to help you implement Morning Meeting and assess your practice.

• **Common Questions**—The questions and answers in these sections address some concerns and issues teachers commonly encounter as their experience with Morning Meeting evolves. If questions come up for you as you read a chapter or as you use Morning Meeting, look in this section for help. Also, check out the other Morning Meeting resources listed on page 188 and at www.responsive-classroom.org.

• **Ideas**—Ideas for each component help readers visualize what each component might look like in action. The examples shared address a variety of learning needs, which are captured through quick reference grids designed to support planning. You can use these ideas as written, adapt them to meet the needs of the students you teach, or use them as a springboard for creating your own ideas. These ideas can be implemented in kindergarten through sixth grade classrooms and address a range of academic and social-emotional learning goals.

An Overview of
Morning Meeting

It's almost 8:30 on a winter morning and students from the last-to-arrive bus are entering the classroom, hanging their coats, and reading the morning message that their teacher, Ms. Suretti, has written to them. Students who arrived earlier are working at a variety of tasks: some are writing entries in their journals; some are at computer stations practicing math facts; some are quizzing each other on the week's spelling words.

Ms. Suretti turns from her post near the door where she has been greeting students, picks up a chime from the bookshelf nearby, and strikes it gently with a mallet. When the quiet hum in the room has turned to silence and everyone's eyes are on her, she says, "It's Morning Meeting time. Put away what you are working on and come to the rug."

The students in this classroom are about to begin their day of learning by assembling as a community to participate in a Morning Meeting. This predictable routine provides an anchor at the beginning of the day. No matter how students started their own individual days, the class will officially gather together and begin their shared day of learning with Morning Meeting.

By taking the time for Morning Meeting, the teacher provides the predictability students and teachers crave, especially at the start of the day. She also sets the group up for a successful day with a thoughtful meeting that sets the tone for the day and reflects the unique style and needs of this individual teacher and group.

The Morning Meeting ritual will lead the class successfully from the start of the year to the end of the year as they weather the ebbs and flows—August's new supplies and anxious, careful faces; December's prevacation excitement; February's endless colds and coughs; April's spring-has-sprung exuberance. It is this mixture of routine and surprise, of comfort and challenge, that makes Morning Meeting a treasured and flexible teaching practice.

What Is Morning Meeting?

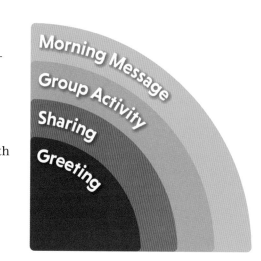

Morning Meeting is a predictable, fun, and engaging way to start each day, build a strong sense of community, and set children up for social, emotional, and academic success. Each morning, students and teachers gather together as a class in a circle for twenty to thirty minutes and interact with one another during four purposeful components:

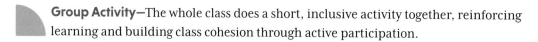

Greeting—Students greet each other by name, often with a handshake, song or chant, or movement.

Sharing—Students share some news or information about themselves and respond to each other, articulating their thoughts, feelings, and ideas in a positive way.

Group Activity—The whole class does a short, inclusive activity together, reinforcing learning and building class cohesion through active participation.

Morning Message—Students practice academic skills and warm up for the day ahead by reading and discussing a daily note posted by their teacher.

The components intentionally provide opportunities for students to practice the skills of greeting, listening and responding, group problem-solving, and noticing and anticipating. Daily practice of the four components gradually weaves a web that binds a class together. Daily Morning Meeting gives students a consistent time and place every day to explore and practice social skills and to merge social, emotional, and academic learning. At the same time, it nurtures empathy by offering students an opportunity to practice taking care of others.

Morning Meeting Format

The Morning Meeting described in this book has a unique set of characteristics and logistical considerations that create the overall experience.

- Morning Meeting rules and procedures are posted in the meeting area.

- Students sit in an evenly spaced circle; the teacher makes sure students practice sitting next to everyone, not just their friends.

- Students come empty-handed.

- The four components are performed in the following order: (1) greeting, (2) sharing, (3) group activity, and (4) morning message.

- Morning Meeting is relatively short: twenty to thirty minutes, depending on students' ages.

- A management signal (such as a chime or raised hand) is taught and used to bring quiet and attention.

This format, along with the four discrete components, sets it apart from other types of community gatherings. (See the Getting Started section on page 22 for ways to create a Morning Meeting experience that reflects this format.)

Why Morning Meeting Matters

Our increasingly global twenty-first century society, marked by rapid innovation and change, has engendered widespread acknowledgment that students need, more than ever, to develop strong cognitive abilities and social and emotional proficiencies. Morning Meeting nurtures and provides a place to develop and practice all of these skills.

Among the competencies needed for success in the twenty-first century are the abilities to communicate ideas and information clearly; to collaborate; to demonstrate innovation and think flexibly; and to analyze, synthesize, and evaluate information from diverse sources. Of equal importance are the skills of responsible citizenship. The world we live in requires citizens who can learn from and work collaboratively with others from diverse cultures (Bellanca and Brandt 2010). Strong communication and cross-cultural skills are essential to meeting this goal.

Threaded through our common understanding of the need for these competencies is a growing sense of the value of social-emotional skills. Center for Responsive Schools bases all of its programs on the belief that in order for students to achieve success both in and out of school, they need to learn five specific social-emotional competencies, namely, cooperation, assertiveness, responsibility, empathy, and self-control, or C.A.R.E.S.

Social-Emotional Competencies and Definitions

 Cooperation—Students' ability to establish new relationships, maintain positive relationships and friendships, avoid social isolation, resolve conflicts, accept differences, be a contributing member of the classroom and school community, and work productively and collaboratively with others.

 Assertiveness—Students' ability to take initiative, stand up for their ideas without hurting or negating others, seek help, succeed at a challenging task, and recognize their individual self as separate from the circumstances or conditions they're in.

 Responsibility—Students' ability to motivate themselves to take action and follow through on expectations; to define a problem, consider the consequences, and choose a positive solution.

 Empathy—Students' ability to "see into" (recognize, understand) another's state of mind and emotions and be receptive to new ideas and perspectives; to appreciate and value differences and diversity in others; to have concern for others' welfare, even when it doesn't benefit or may come as a cost to oneself.

 Self-Control—Students' ability to recognize and regulate their thoughts, emotions, and behaviors in order to be successful in the moment and remain on a successful trajectory.

Research confirms the long-held conviction of many educators regarding the critical importance of these social-emotional skills and their connection to academic progress. One group of researchers analyzed over 200 studies and found that students who receive SEL instruction had more positive attitudes about school and improved an average of eleven percentile points on standardized achievement tests compared to students who did not receive such instruction (Durlak et al. 2011).

Purposes and Goals of Morning Meeting

A person who can demonstrate self-control and listen well, who can frame a thoughtful question and pose it respectfully, and who can examine a situation from a number of perspectives will be a stronger learner. All those skills—so essential to academic achievement—can be modeled, experienced, practiced, extended, and refined in the context of social interaction. And Morning Meeting provides a forum in which this integration of social interaction and skill development can occur. The Morning Meeting components also offer students endless opportunities to practice academic skills—whether counting by twos, using vocabulary words correctly, or reviewing newly learned geology concepts—in a safe and energizing way.

> **A well-crafted, purposeful Morning Meeting:**
>
> - Sets a tone for respectful and engaged learning in a climate of trust
>
> - Builds and enhances connections among students and between students and teachers
>
> - Merges academic, social, and emotional learning
>
> - Motivates students by addressing the human needs to feel a sense of significance and belonging and to have fun
>
> - Through the repetition of many ordinary moments of respectful interaction, enables some extraordinary moments

Setting the Tone for Respectful and Engaged Learning

Beginnings can be critical. We can all remember the feeling of joining a group and not being quite sure whom we would connect with, whom we could talk to, how we would fit in, and if we felt a sense of trust. Once we settled in, the details most likely drifted from our cluttered memory, but the pace and feeling of the beginning likely influenced the way we felt at the end of the day and whether the day's challenges had been exhilarating or overwhelming.

The same is true for our students: beginnings matter. The way we begin each day in our classroom sets the tone for learning and speaks volumes about what and whom we value, about our expectations for the way we will treat each other, and about the way we believe learning occurs.

Students' learning begins the second they walk through the doors of the building. Children notice whether they are greeted warmly or overlooked, whether the classroom feels chaotic and unpredictable or ordered and comforting. If they announce, "My cat got hit by a car last night, but it's gonna be all right," they may find an interested, supportive audience or one that turns away. Every detail of their experience informs students about the classroom and their place in it.

When we start the day with everyone together, face-to-face, welcoming each person, sharing news, listening to individual voices, and communicating as a caring group, we make several powerful statements. We say that every person counts. We say that the way we interact individually and as a group is significant. We say that our classroom culture is one of friendliness and thoughtfulness. We say that we can accomplish hard work and make important discoveries together. We say that teachers hold authority, even though they are a part of the circle. We say that this is a place where courtesy and warmth and safety reign—a place of respect for all.

To learn, we must take risks—offering up a tentative answer we are far from sure is right or trying out a new part in the chorus when we are not sure we can hit the notes. We are more willing to take these risks when we know we will be respected and valued, no matter the outcome. To risk, we must trust, and Morning Meeting helps create a climate of trust.

When we hold Morning Meeting consistently over time, we see the friendly, respectful behaviors established in the circle overflow beyond it. We overhear students talking at lunch about a common interest discovered during a Morning Meeting sharing, forging the beginning of a new friendship. Children may start to greet each other spontaneously at the start of the day, even before Morning Meeting begins.

A first grade teacher whose class had been using Morning Meeting for several months wrote: "One Tuesday as I stood by the door, waiting for the class to gather, I just watched. They were genuinely glad to see each other. Some were hugging as they greeted each other. Some were clapping for something. What a joy to watch—I was merely an observer and just loved it."

Building Connections Between All Members of the Classroom

Feeling connected to a school community is an important factor in students' success. Students who feel connected to school report that they like school, feel they belong, have friends at school, and believe their teachers care about them and their learning. Attendance improves along with students' motivation and engagement with learning (Blum 2005).

Morning Meeting helps to create and extend connections among all members of the classroom community. Each component helps children to know others and to be known. Greeting, for example, begins with the very basic element of learning and using each other's names. Sharing helps students learn details about each other's experiences, preferences, and interests, as well as those of their teachers. Picture Kezziah, who loves knowing that her teacher, Mr. Russell, likes snakes too, and has a pet boa constrictor. Or imagine the connections that form when a query the teacher has embedded in the morning message prompts students to gather and graph information about the people in their family. Reading the message, Jeremy learns that Gavin lives with his grandmother too, and Amari and Hannah learn that they both have two moms. All these personal connections can help children feel acknowledged and motivated to learn.

The opportunity for positive connection that Morning Meeting provides is just as important in the upper grades as in the lower ones. Students in grades four through six are entering preadolescence, a time marked by tumultuous emotional, physical, and cognitive changes. Morning Meeting enables these older students to do what they most want and need to do: interact with their peers.

Older students long to be part of the group, but they're often not quite sure how to join together in a way that doesn't exclude others. The four components of Morning Meeting allow students to connect with their peers in a safe, positive, and inclusive way. Through the structures of Morning Meeting they can learn how to turn their need for peer connection into a positive and dynamic learning strategy.

In addition to helping individuals within the classroom community to know each other better, Morning Meeting helps build cultural knowledge and appreciation. Each classroom represents a unique community of students and families, and Morning Meeting offers many ways that we can take advantage of the diversity inherent in every group. We can help the class learn and use greetings in different languages and, in the process, make connections to various students' family origins. Topics for sharing can include information about families' favorite foods, games, and traditions. Sometimes games that are shared can become group activities. Cross-cultural understanding and competence develop as students share information from their own lives and learn about those of their classmates.

Finally, the practice of observing and interacting with students in Morning Meeting gives teachers an opportunity to garner important information that can help them differentiate instruction to respond to the needs and strengths of individual students. For example, what we learn in Morning Meeting can help as we choose books that might capture a reluctant reader's interests or assign partners for a science project.

Merging Academic and Social-Emotional Learning

Morning Meeting provides ample daily opportunities for children to review information learned in content areas and practice skills specific to those areas. For example, an activity might draw on recently learned math skills or a morning message might ask children to correct capitalization errors.

But perhaps more importantly, the respectful, inclusive setting of Morning Meeting harnesses the innate synergy among academic, social, and emotional learning. As social beings, we learn through dialogue with others—and this is true for all subject areas. We extend our knowledge, test our assumptions, confirm or revise our thoughts, and generate questions that will lead to a new iteration of ideas. Observing, reflecting, speaking, and listening are fundamental to our ability to learn. These skills enable us to exchange perspectives and ideas, explain our thinking, and critique the thinking of others—skills that children need for success in all areas of school and life.

Increasingly, people are acknowledging the role that dialogue plays in promoting academic growth. According to research conducted by the ACS Centre for Inspiring Minds, "69% of the students surveyed believe that speaking or listening is the most important academic skill (over reading or writing). However, 73% reported receiving the least amount of classroom instruction on how to effectively speak or listen; research on language use has shown that approximately 40% of class time should be used in dialogue in order to maximise effective learning" (cited by Talking in Class 2015).

Morning Meeting provides a daily arena for "rich, structured conversations" in which social, emotional, and academic learning is an integrated experience, full of chances to develop foundational thinking and language skills such as listening attentively, speaking clearly, asking purposeful questions, answering thoughtfully, giving reasons for assertions, and agreeing and disagreeing respectfully.

A group activity—Mystery Word (page 133)—from a lively Morning Meeting in Ms. Franklin's second grade classroom provides a great example:

> "Our activity today is Mystery Word," Ms. Franklin announces. The students lean forward eagerly as she holds up a handful of neatly lettered oaktag cards she has prepared. Each tag has on it one word from an article titled "Superstorms" that the class read the previous day. A tornado, rare in their area, touched down in a neighboring town a few months earlier, affecting many people they knew, and students' interest in the topic is keen. After quickly summarizing the article with the class, reviewing some key details, and confirming that everyone is familiar with the words on the cards, Ms. Franklin says to the class, "Ready to start? Isaiah, your turn to go first."
>
> As Isaiah stands and closes his eyes, Ms. Franklin makes a show of shuffling the cards and then tapes one to his back. Slowly, with his back turned to his classmates to display his mystery word, he sidles around the inside of the circle. His classmates will offer clues to him—"in complete sentences," reminds their teacher—until he guesses the word correctly.
>
> "When the tornado came, it blanked a lot of trees," the first clue-giver says.

"Destroyed?" Isaiah guesses.

"Well, that would work, but it's not the word."

"Sometimes when a tree gets blanked it doesn't live anymore," comes the next clue.

Isaiah stands, thinking hard. "Uh, uprooted?"

A resounding "Yes!" from the whole circle celebrates his response, and round two begins.

This activity is rich with the reinforcement of academic content and practice in listening and speaking skills. Students use content vocabulary, follow directions, take turns, practice patient, respectful listening, use complete sentences, and delight in each other's success. The article and its vocabulary will be fresh in their minds later in the day when they begin writing stories connected to the topic. This conversation and activity sharpen the tools of listening and speaking that are essential for partner chats, small-group discussions, peer critiquing, and other cooperative learning strategies. The preamble and the activity itself take perhaps ten minutes—ten precious minutes of rapt engagement with the curriculum and each other.

Addressing the Human Needs for Belonging, Significance, and Fun

All of us need to feel that we belong and are valued for the competencies, skills, and knowledge we bring to a group. We need to feel that our unique contributions are recognized and appreciated. All the components of Morning Meeting address those needs directly.

Former *Responsive Classroom* educational consultant Melissa Correa-Connolly speaks of what she has seen happen, both in her own classroom and in the rooms of many teachers with whom she has worked:

> I think of Morning Meeting as having such immense power because it meets the emotional needs of children. It acknowledges everyone and makes them feel significant. It does away with the feeling many children have of being a piece of furniture in the classroom. Morning Meeting is the first thing in the morning, and it allows children to be seen and to have a voice.

Having fun is also a universal human need. Fun does not necessarily mean frivolity or silliness; it does mean engagement and fascination with what we do. An activity can be fun and playful even when it's a great challenge. Having fun is not about winning but about immersion in the pleasure of the activity itself.

Fun might involve striving to find the five punctuation errors planted in the morning message or learning to sing a song with motions. It might mean trying to guess the three-digit number a classmate is thinking of in the game Pica Ferme Nada (page 134). Fun might mean learning a new and lively greeting E. J. brought back from summer camp or laughing along with Amy when she reports on her new puppy's antics. Fun is also connected with risk-taking. Risks taken in a playful way can teach us how to handle the more serious risks that growth can demand.

One thing is certain: humans strive to fulfill their needs in whatever way they can, whether those ways are positive or negative. The student who isn't recognized in the group for friendly contributions may become known for their trouble-making contributions. When school doesn't provide constructive ways to meet students' need for fun, students may devise their own, often not-so-constructive or inclusive ways.

Morning Meeting is full of opportunities for a class to have fun together and for all its members to feel a sense of significance and belonging, needs widely affirmed by educational theory and research: "Adler (1930) proposed that a sense of belonging motivates children to develop their skills and contribute to the welfare of all . . . Research indicates that educators who establish firm boundaries, foster warm personal relationships in the classroom, and enable students to have an impact on their environment strengthen students' attachment to their school, their interest in learning, their ability to refrain from self-destructive behaviors, and their positive behaviors" (Elias et al. 1997).

Enabling Extraordinary Moments

Morning Meeting, repeated every day, is full of moments that by themselves may seem quite mundane. But this repetition can enable some quite extraordinary moments within the meeting circle. For example, the habits of participation established by Morning Meeting routines can serve a community well in very difficult circumstances. Teacher Joyce Love's experience testifies to this.

By taking part in Morning Meeting, her class had learned how to come quickly together and how to listen respectfully to each other. They had considered hard questions, such as "What can you say when someone shares something that's really upsetting to them?" as well as "What might we say when someone shares something that makes them really happy?" They had, under Joyce's guidance, carefully constructed habits of participation and practiced them day in and day out in the most ordinary situations with the most ordinary news—a swimming test passed, a baby brother with chicken pox, a visit from relatives.

One morning, several of Joyce's students saw a dead body on a street corner on their walk to school. Now, when they were confronted with an event of monumental impact, they had a familiar circle to come to. They had patterns of sharing and response that their teacher could draw on to help them deal with a haunting scene. "If it hadn't been for Morning Meeting, I wouldn't have known what to do," Joyce recalled. "Its structures helped take care of things."

Morning Meeting also helps when students are affected by the news of difficult events that have occurred in the larger world, whether it's an earthquake that left thousands homeless or a bomb blast that killed many. The established, predictable format of the meeting is familiar and com-

forting during disturbing times. In addition, having all students gathered in a circle allows the teacher to notice any whose distress seems acute and who might need extra attention or support beyond the classroom. And perhaps most importantly, the very restoration of routine sends a powerful message that helps to model and build resilience: hard things happen, we acknowledge them, and we continue on.

Thankfully, not all extraordinary moments are tragic ones. Consider this story told by a teacher from a school where Morning Meeting was an established part of school life in all the classrooms:

> One wintry Tuesday morning at about 9:30, just as Morning Meeting in my room was ending, a second grader from the classroom adjacent to mine entered and approached me politely. "Excuse me, Mrs. Truesdell, but our teacher isn't here yet. We finished Morning Meeting, but we don't know what to do next."
>
> A series of missed communications involving a school secretary with the flu and a faulty answering machine had resulted in a class without a teacher or a substitute. These seven-year-olds knew the routines so well that they had gathered themselves and conducted an orderly and merry Morning Meeting. I remembered, in fact, hearing the strains of the song "River" wafting through the thin wall that connected the two rooms and thinking how much better it sounded than last week!

These children's daily participation in the ongoing routines of Morning Meeting had enabled them to take responsibility for these routines even in the absence of their teacher. Their school celebrated their responsible behavior at an assembly later that week.

Getting Started

When educators hear about Morning Meeting and see or experience it in action, they are often excited to get started. They want to dive right in to the process of mapping out their meetings and trying them out. While Morning Meeting is a relatively easy structure to follow once you are familiar with its components, there are some key considerations to keep in mind as you prepare to get the most out of the Morning Meeting experience.

Establish a Set Schedule

Ideally, Morning Meeting happens every day, first thing in the morning. The length of the meeting is important—plan on twenty to thirty minutes. If the meeting is much shorter than twenty minutes, achieving the desired social-emotional and academic goals is difficult. If the meeting is too long, students become restless and the meeting loses impact.

Of course, a Morning Meeting may need to be shorter than twenty minutes on days with special events such as field trips, guest speakers, or school assemblies. You might do all four components but keep each one brief. Alternatively, you could do just two components, such as greeting and morning message. This would maintain the routine and set the tone for the day.

When administrators create school schedules they should consider how to reserve twenty to thirty minutes each day for all classrooms. This might mean that nobody moves to special areas or services for the first forty-five minutes after the school day officially begins. This allows time for students to be welcomed into the classroom and participate in a full Morning Meeting before

Time Well Spent

Teachers must commit more than just time to implement Morning Meeting successfully. They must also commit themselves to a belief in children's capacity to take care of themselves and each other as they learn academic skills (like vocabulary and algorithms) and social-emotional skills (like respect, responsibility, and stretching the boundaries of their social world). Besides creating opportunities for students to practice such skills, Morning Meeting also creates opportunities for teachers to model these skills and give children valuable feedback.

The time teachers commit to Morning Meeting is an investment that is repaid many times over. The sense of belonging and the skills of attention, listening, expression, and cooperative interaction developed in Morning Meeting are a foundation for every lesson, every transition time, every lining up, every handling of an upset or conflict, all day and all year long.

moving from their primary classroom. Classroom teachers who have very tight schedules should consider how the components of the Morning Meeting might support the remainder of the day and save time introducing a lesson or potentially minimizing time lost to off-task behavior. For example, if students have a math test, Mental Math Pushups (page 132) might be a great activity for review and save time that would otherwise be needed for the review. Or if students have to work with partners in a science experiment, setting up a partner chat during the sharing component of Morning Meeting and modeling how to work with a partner might save time needed for the experiment.

In some schools, upper elementary grades begin the structure of changing classes a few times a day. Finding time to schedule Morning Meeting can be challenging in these situations. If possible, collaborate with team members and other colleagues to find an optimal solution. Here are some ideas:

- Do Morning Meeting three times a week during advisory or homeroom. Much of the benefit of Morning Meeting comes from repeated practice of social-emotional and academic skills. If Morning Meeting is only an occasional event, not only is its impact diminished but it's also likely that the meeting itself will be less successful since students won't have developed the skills necessary to reap the intended benefits of the meeting. It's important, therefore, to schedule Morning Meeting to occur several times a week, if possible on the same days, so that students can count on a predictable structure. On days when you don't do a full Morning Meeting, you might do two components—perhaps greeting and morning message. Or you might plan advisory or homeroom activities that reinforce skills such as respectful listening and questioning, self-control, focused presentation, and cooperative learning. For example, you could schedule peer tutoring, service learning projects, or team-building activities.

- Do portions of Morning Meeting at other times of the day. If you need to do an abbreviated Morning Meeting first thing in the morning, you could incorporate the missed portions into other parts of the day. For example, you could do sharing as an energizer during an academic lesson, after silent reading, or at closing circle at the end of the day.

- Do all of Morning Meeting at a different time of day. Although it's best if Morning Meeting comes at the beginning of the day, it's not always possible. Some schools have advisory during second period. In that case, that's when Morning Meeting might take place. If your school doesn't have an advisory or homeroom period, you may have to look for a consistent segment of time such as a sustained silent reading or study hall.

- Switch up the adult leading the meeting by trading classes and leading Morning Meeting in classes that you traditionally see at a different time of the day. Having the adults switch places once a week to run a Morning Meeting in a class teachers might not see until second or third period helps them build relationships will all the groups of students they see throughout the day.

Consider the Space and Setup

One of the first things to think about when planning for Morning Meeting is the space where you'll hold it. You'll want to create a space large enough for all participants to sit in an even circle so that all can see and be seen—this is an essential element of the meeting. Many teachers set this space off with a colorful carpet or carpet squares to indicate, "This is our gathering spot."

Creating this space can present challenges in small or oddly shaped classrooms, but it's worth persevering. Holding Morning Meeting in an elongated oval or amoeba shape can result in some students feeling unnoticed and disengaged, which works against one of the purposes of Morning Meeting: to welcome all into the classroom and build community. Sometimes, having a colleague look at your space with you can be helpful—a fresh set of eyes might see ways you can reconfigure the space. (For ideas on creating meeting spaces, see *Empowering Educators: A Comprehensive Guide to Teaching Grades K, 1, 2* and *Empowering Educators: A Comprehensive Guide to Teaching Grades 3, 4, 5*, published by Center for Responsive Schools.)

You'll also want to think about whether students will sit on the floor or in chairs. This decision will depend partly on students' developmental needs. Many students sit quite happily on the floor; others seem to handle themselves better, or feel recognized as being more mature, when seated in chairs. Some students simply need the physical support of chairs. One teacher of fifth graders began the year by having students sit on the floor for Morning Meeting and had to repeatedly remind them to sit up. After realizing that they were going through tremendous growth spurts and were physically uncomfortable on the floor, the teacher was able to remedy the situation by switching to chairs.

Lay the Groundwork

In the first days of school, it's important to spend some time helping students get ready for successful participation in Morning Meeting. This preparation includes teaching and modeling basic routines such as how to come to the meeting circle, teaching a signal for quiet, briefly introducing the purpose of Morning Meeting, and presenting or creating meeting rules. Laying this groundwork doesn't take a lot of time and is a crucial step for ongoing success with Morning Meeting. In the following sections, you'll find how-to information on each of these topics.

Carefully Teach Procedures and Routines

Over and over in our teaching lives, we are reminded not to make assumptions about what students know. This applies to daily classroom routines just as it applies to academic content. Many routines contribute to Morning Meeting running smoothly. Perhaps you'll want everyone to bring chairs to the circle or move furniture around to create room for a circle. Once in the circle, students need to know how to sit with empty, quiet hands and how to listen attentively. Plus, each component of Morning Meeting has its own routines—how to greet someone respectfully, how to share information, how to move safely during an activity. These routines require careful instruction at the outset and vigilant monitoring even after they have been established.

Coming Together in a Circle

Throughout history and across cultures, people have come together in a circle to build, enhance, and celebrate community. Whether telling stories around a fire or performing a sacred ritual, gathering together in a circle taps into our sense of connection and shared humanity—and bringing students together in a circle during Morning Meeting does the same. While sitting or standing in a circle, students can see one another, which helps them actively listen to and respond to one another and build a sense of community and belonging. In addition, this format encourages participation and makes it easier for the teacher to gauge students' understanding and adjust instruction or conversation topics accordingly. The circle environment allows everyone to feel like equals—everyone sitting or standing together, the same distance apart, without hierarchy.

Use Consistent Signals

One of the most essential procedures to teach students from the very beginning of the school year is how you'll get their attention. Having simple, effective signals to get students' quiet attention is key to establishing a productive classroom community and a smoothly run Morning Meeting. Raising your voice may be simple but is rarely effective, and if students are involved in conversations or activities, chances are that many will not absorb the announcement.

Instead, you can use various nonverbal signals that say to students, "Stop what you are doing and give me [or a student who may be about to speak] your attention." To call students to the meeting circle, an auditory signal such as a chime, bell, or triangle or a visual signal such as dimming the lights might be most effective. When you have the attention of all students, make a brief statement: "Five minutes till Morning Meeting. Put away what you are working on and come to the meeting area."

When students are gathered in the meeting circle, a hands-up signal is useful to get their quiet attention. Suppose it is Jonas's turn to share. He has brought a picture of his new hamster, Harry, but has left it in his desk. When Jonas leaves the circle to get the picture, his classmates start chatting. Jonas comes back, ready to share, but his classmates continue to talk. The teacher, Mrs. Regules, raises her hand. Across the circle, Amanda notices and raises hers. Around the circle, hands go up as the signal spreads and silence follows. It is simple and efficient, with not a word of scolding or blame. His audience is ready, and Jonas begins. "This is a picture of Harry. He likes eating cucumbers . . ."

Students will benefit from formal, structured teaching and practice of classroom routines. On the facing page is an example of Interactive Modeling, a way for students to learn these routines. In the example, Mrs. Regules, the teacher, follows up her instruction by deliberately cueing her students to put the behavior into action during real classroom work while she observes and coaches. After she has completed the steps of Interactive Modeling, she says, "We'll keep using this signal throughout the day today."

> ## At the Circle With Empty Hands
>
> Students come empty-handed to the meeting so they can focus without distractions, but also because they—their points of view, insights, experiences, and the words they use to paint a picture—are enough. While students may share objects such as work products or photos, this should not be a required part of the sharing experience and should be done sparingly. In those cases, the objects remain to the side until it is time for sharing. The rest of the time, sharing the space, ideas, and experience is the priority of the sharing component.

Later, when she sees students successfully responding to the signal during a social studies activity, she says, "Everyone quickly finished their conversations when they saw me raise my hand, and lots of people helped spread the signal so everyone could see it. That helps us work together as a community!"

Introduce Morning Meeting to Students

If students are new to Morning Meeting, begin by establishing their prior knowledge about meetings. You might ask, "What are some kinds of meetings you know about—meetings that you, your family members, or someone else you know have been to? What kinds of things happened at those meetings?" After students share their ideas and experiences, let them know that they'll begin each day with a meeting called Morning Meeting. Describe the meeting and tell them your hopes and goals for this part of the day. Your list might sound something like this:

- I hope that we will all get to know one another—not just our best friends or the people we hang out with all the time—so that everyone will feel that they're part of our classroom community.

- I want us to be able to share different experiences and ideas.

- I want us to learn and have fun together as a group.

If students are already familiar with Morning Meeting from previous years, ask them to name their hopes and goals for this part of the day.

Often, teachers of older students worry that Morning Meeting may seem babyish, particularly if students remember doing it in first and second grade. Emphasize the amount of peer interaction that will occur during Morning Meeting—something that older students crave as their peer group

Interactive Modeling

Interactive Modeling is a useful strategy for teaching many different signals and procedures. It starts with the teacher modeling a desired action or behavior and then actively involving students in observing and practicing the behavior in order to better grasp and remember it. Here are the steps of Interactive Modeling as they might be used to teach a signal for quiet attention:

Say what you will model and why. "When I need to get your attention in the meeting circle or other places, one of the signals I'll use is raising my hand."

Model the behavior. Mrs. Regules asks for a volunteer to raise their hand. "Penelope is going to raise her hand, and I'm going to respond. Notice what I do." Mrs. Regules begins talking, and Penelope raises her hand. Mrs. Regules quickly finishes her thought and then raises her own hand as she quietly turns her attention to Penelope.

Ask students what they noticed. Students respond, "You finished what you were saying," "You turned your body and looked at Penelope," and "You raised your hand too."

Invite one or more students to model. Several students volunteer. "This time, Julie and Kwame will model having a conversation, and Luis will raise his hand." The class watches as the students model the behavior.

Again, ask students what they noticed. Students say what they saw and heard. "Kwame finished telling Julie about the pie he baked with his dad yesterday, but then he stopped"; "Julie looked up when she saw the signal, but then she let Kwame finish his sentence"; "Julie nodded and smiled, but she didn't add anything else." "What did she do?" asks the teacher. "She stayed quiet."

Have all students practice. "Now, let's all practice," Mrs. Regules says. "Partner up with someone sitting near you and talk for a minute about something you did over the summer, and then I'll raise my hand."

Provide feedback. "I saw people listening respectfully as their partners finished their stories, then turn their attention to me. We'll have lots of opportunities to keep practicing each day!"

(For more on Interactive Modeling, see *Interactive Modeling: A Powerful Technique for Teaching Children* by Margaret Berry Wilson, published by Center for Responsive Schools.)

becomes more and more important. And reassure them that you will plan meetings that reflect their interests and draw from their curriculum. Your enthusiastic introduction of Morning Meeting and careful planning can go a long way toward making Morning Meeting a success for older elementary students.

Establish Morning Meeting Ground Rules

From the very beginning, it is important to establish some ground rules and procedures that will help Morning Meeting run smoothly. These can be teacher generated or created collaboratively with the class. In either case, the ground rules should be few in number and stated positively—these rules are helpful guideposts for behavior, not harsh prohibitions.

If you choose to work with the class to create meeting rules, begin the process with a question such as "To make our Morning Meeting respectful, safe, and fun, what rules will we need?" This question helps students stay focused on the purpose of rules: to maintain safety and order for all.

Answers are likely to include variations of these rules:

- Listen to the speaker.
- Look at the person who's talking.
- Keep your body in control.
- Raise your hand if you want to talk.
- Keep your hand down when someone is speaking.
- Make room for everyone in the circle.
- Offer thoughtful questions and comments.

Because a long list of rules can be difficult to follow, edit this list down to three to five essential rules that encompass all the details named. For example:

- Listen respectfully.
- Be welcoming to everyone.
- Be ready to participate.

Post the rules near the Morning Meeting space so that students can refer to them frequently. With both teacher-created and cocreated rules, it's important to discuss and model the rules over the first few weeks of doing Morning Meeting so that students have a concrete understanding of what following the rules looks like and sounds like.

In a fifth grade class, the teacher leads a discussion of what it means to "be respectful." "How do people show respect in a meeting?" she asks. In a kindergarten class, one of the meeting rules is "Listen to each other." "How will someone who's speaking know that you're listening?" the teacher asks. In both classrooms, discussions ensue on the finer points of listening etiquette and respectful meeting behavior. Each teacher then uses Interactive Modeling to demonstrate and have students practice these behaviors.

Start Simply and Increase Complexity Over Time

Many teachers, particularly those of older elementary students, find that they can successfully hold a complete but simple Morning Meeting on the first day of school. Others might just do a greeting on the first day and phase in the other components over the next few days.

The goal is to incorporate all four components as soon as students are ready. Factors such as students' ages and levels of school experience and your knowledge of the particular group of students you're teaching will influence how quickly you phase in components. Give students the time and space to grow into the Morning Meeting experience so that it remains joyful. Listen and watch your students; they will show you what they need.

Redirecting Behavior During Morning Meeting

Keep the goal of community in mind as you implement Morning Meeting. If students' attention is starting to wane and redirection is taking up more time than the meeting itself, close the meeting and then do the other components throughout the day. After, think about what structures might meet the needs of students for the following day or where students might be better placed for support.

Too many redirections within the circle setting of the Morning Meeting can inadvertently send the signal to the group that a student or group of students are trouble and should be avoided. When the goal is to see and be seen, we want to ensure all students are seen in the best light.

In the early days of school, keep all components simple, highly structured, and low risk, even in classrooms where students are familiar with Morning Meeting from previous years. Choose greetings and activities that are straightforward and easy to manage, carefully structure sharing, and focus your message on one task. For example, in a first Morning Meeting with fourth graders, you might do an Interview greeting (page 68), which combines greeting and sharing, followed by Take Sides (page 135) for the group activity, and end with a simple morning message to get students thinking about what they are looking forward to in fourth grade.

As a sense of positive community gets established and students get to know each other better, you can introduce more high-risk elements. Of course, what feels risky can change throughout the year depending on emerging issues, events, or developmental needs. Low-risk elements are often needed later in the year for a variety of reasons—for example, students need to revisit a skill, the class needs a calming greeting on an exciting day, or an element coming up later in that day's Morning Meeting is high risk. Similarly, high-risk elements can work well early in the school year if students have already demonstrated success with simpler activities. (For more information about increasing the complexity of individual components, see the Getting Started sections in the chapters that follow.)

Do the Components in Order

The order of the four components—greeting, sharing, group activity, and morning message—matters. Once you've taught all four components, stick to this order. Greeting serves as a logical warm-up and tone-setter for sharing, which requires that students feel a sense of comfort and trust in the group. For sharing to work well, the group must be feeling settled and calm. When teachers try doing sharing after group activity, they often notice that students aren't able to listen well or ask focused and thoughtful questions.

Group activity follows sharing because at this point in the meeting children are ready for the invigoration of whole-group involvement. Morning message helps to bring the group back to a calmer mood after the liveliness of the activity and serves as a transition to the rest of the school day.

Plan Meetings Purposefully

A rich and meaningful Morning Meeting does not happen by accident. Just as with lessons, a teacher needs to plan Morning Meetings purposefully, considering several factors:

- **How Much Time You Have**—Determine how much time you have for Morning Meeting on a given day and choose ideas for each component accordingly. If you choose a longer greeting and activity, choose a shorter sharing and morning message so that everything fits into your twenty-to thirty-minute time frame.

- **How to Incorporate Elements From the Curriculum**—Figure out ways to integrate skills, concepts, and ideas from the academic curriculum into the meetings. For example, for a third grade language arts class beginning a unit on mysteries, you might choose Alibi (page 123) as a group activity. This game would give students a fun way to use key vocabulary from the unit. For fifth graders who are studying energy in science, you could do an around-the-circle sharing about a recent time when students noticed energy in use. Students could then sort the examples into categories of different kinds of energy.

Being Responsive to Student Needs

In order to meet the goals of the Morning Meeting, the meetings should reflect the unique nature of the classroom community. When designing the meeting, it is important to consider academic, social, and emotional goals. For example, if a class struggled to work cooperatively in a science experiment, the teacher might stop the experiment and shift gears to work in a text. Then during Morning Meeting the following day, the teacher might choose activities that will require cooperation so she can draw upon those lessons later in the day as she reattempts the experiment.

It is also important to consider how all students will be seen and have a sense of belonging and significance. As you get to know your class, think about what types of meetings will meet these diverse needs. A teacher who has a nonverbal learner may look for sharing ideas with visuals where students make connections through chosen classroom signals. Incorporating these options allows for all students to meet the goals of the sharing and feel connected to the classroom community.

- **Which Social-Emotional Skills Students Need to Practice**—What are students' social-emotional strengths and challenges? Where are they in their development? What are some recent challenges that they would benefit from working on? For example, a fifth grade teacher observed the formation of cliques and knew that some students were feeling excluded at various times during the day. As part of her effort to address this, she decided to focus on team building in the next Morning Meeting and chose a greeting, sharing, and activity that had students interact with many different classmates.

- **The Mood of the Class**—Is the class preoccupied by certain current events? Is a holiday affecting their ability to focus? Sometimes these are things you can plan for. For example, on the morning after Halloween, the selected content and structure of the meeting may need to be low-key and calming. You might plan in advance to use a simple seated greeting and a focused partner sharing on "What I did last night." At other times, you may need to make a quick change to the plan after assessing students as they walk through the door. For example, on a grey Monday morning when students seem sleepy, you may need to select more invigorating content, like the One-Minute greeting (page 70) and a round of Aroostasha (page 124) for the group activity.

The thought of planning for yet another "subject" may seem overwhelming. "I hardly have enough time to plan for the core subjects that I'm required to teach," one fourth grade teacher lamented to her teaching partner when she first began implementing Morning Meeting. But as they planned together, they began to discover ways to integrate the curriculum into Morning Meeting. They also created simple planning sheets that directed their thinking and kept them focused on both the goals of Morning Meeting and the life of the classroom, all while keeping the meetings to twenty or thirty minutes. As the year progressed, Morning Meeting became an essential part of the day, rich with opportunities for academic engagement and community building.

Scan the QR code to access daily and weekly Morning Meeting planning guides.

Stay in Control

Make no mistake: running Morning Meeting successfully requires a teacher who is in control. As teachers, we are planners, interpreters, synthesizers, timekeepers, and safety-net holders. Just as we are in charge of lessons in social studies, math, or language arts, we need to stay in charge during Morning Meeting.

What is required of us in this role may be simple and straightforward. "Choose one more person for a question or comment, Danita," we say when many hands are raised and time is running short; "Join the circle, Todd," to a student who tends to hang back.

Other times, discerning and guiding the dynamics in Morning Meeting can be more complex. Nine-year-old Jeremy continually shares complicated details of "scary science" stories about mutant viruses, colliding asteroids, and toxic pesticides that invisibly saturate strawberries. He is highly knowledgeable and his graphic details are accurate and documented.

Jeremy's teacher wonders about the effect of this stream of intense news, so authoritatively presented, on his peers. Are they upset, challenged, or embarrassed by their relative lack of factual knowledge? Is this a positive way for Jeremy to define a niche in the class? Careful observation and perhaps a one-on-one chat with Jeremy outside of Morning Meeting will inform his teacher as she contemplates whether her intervention is needed to protect either him or the class.

Use Teacher Language to Remind Students of Expectations and Reinforce Success

Addressing what can seem like small details—whom students greet, where they sit, which students are rarely the recipients of thoughtful comments—sends two messages: you value the skills and attitudes that specific actions reflect, and you believe in the students' capacity to accomplish these actions.

The language we use as teachers carries a great deal of weight in communicating and holding students to our expectations, as well as encouraging and supporting students' efforts. No matter the purpose, effective teacher language:

- Is clear, simple, and direct

- Is genuine and respectful

- Gives specific positive feedback rather than general praise

- Focuses on the child's action or behavior rather than generalizing about the child's whole person

- Avoids qualitative or personal judgment

- Shows faith in children's ability to follow the rules

There are several different types of teacher language that can support all aspects of school life, including Morning Meeting.

Envisioning language helps students picture positive outcomes for themselves and their learning. For example:

- This year, I look forward to getting to know everyone in the class.

- Today, we're going to do an activity that gets us focused to help us do well on this morning's spelling test.

- Learning each other's names is going to help us form a strong classroom community.

- This week, we get to be explorers as we go on a nature walk around the school!

Reinforcing language names and affirms students' positive behaviors so that they can build on those behaviors. For example:

- I noticed that everyone remembered each other's names during greeting.

- Lots of people are choosing to sit next to different classmates today.

- Most people are remembering to read the message chart when they enter our room in the morning.

- You are giving many specific details to support your ideas in sharing.

Reminding language prompts students to remember established expectations, and it can be used proactively to help children prepare for an activity or reactively as behavior is starting to stray off course. For example:

- What things do you need to remember so everyone feels safe to share their ideas during this activity?

- What will we need to keep in mind if someone makes a mistake during this activity?

- Meeting rules, everyone.

- Laurie, what do you need to remember as you move your chair into the circle?

Redirecting language offers clear, nonnegotiable directions to help students regain control when their behavior gets fully off-task. For example:

- Eyes on the speaker, Natalie.

- All hands down until the speaker is finished.

- Mateo, keep your body in your own space.

- Laurie, you need to walk in this activity.

Give Students Responsibility

Virtually every moment in Morning Meeting is laden with opportunities for students to assume responsibility in the community we call our classroom. Students are responsible for making someone feel welcome, sitting next to a variety of classmates, asking a thoughtful question, making a kind comment, or solving a "puzzler" question on the chart.

In some classrooms, once Morning Meeting is familiar and established, you might also give students supervised responsibilities for specific portions of the meeting. For example, younger children might do well with beginning a greeting or activity. Just be sure you rotate responsibilities evenly.

As students get older, the key to keeping Morning Meetings successful is for the teacher to still be the meeting planner and facilitator but to figure out ways to give class members added responsibility as they show they are ready for it. For example, later in the year when all students are comfortable with the routines of Morning Meeting, you could have students sign up to be Morning Meeting assistants. They could help you explain or model new greetings or activities.

Older students can also help out with Morning Meeting in younger grades, perhaps going into a younger classroom once a week to help model components of the meeting. And you might enlist students at various ages to welcome any new peers who join the class midyear. These ambassadors can teach new students how to do established greetings or activities before each day's meeting so that the newcomers are able to participate fully.

Involve Staff

Since Morning Meeting builds both student-student and adult-student relationships, it helps to involve all the adults students will interact with in a school setting. Inviting support staff such as nurses, office, lunch, transportation and custodial staff, along with paraprofessionoals, special area teachers, and other adults who work within the building to join Morning Meetings, can help both the adults and students see one another in a different light. Then, when students see these individuals in different settings, they have a bond to share other than the sometimes transactional one of delivering papers to the office or moving through the lunch line.

Communicate With Parents

Parents are very supportive of Morning Meeting when they understand its format and goals. But if their first impression is formed from a child's report of "a new game we played at Morning Meeting," they may draw the mistaken conclusion that this is time taken away from learning. Ongoing communication with parents will help them see Morning Meeting for the vital learning time that it is. Here are several ideas for how you can help parents learn about Morning Meeting.

About the Term *Parent*

Students come from a variety of homes with a variety of family structures. Students might be raised by grandparents, siblings, aunts and uncles, foster families, and other caregivers. All of these individuals are to be honored for devoting their time, attention, and love to raising children. It's difficult to find one word that encompasses all these caregivers. In this book, for ease of reading, we use the term *parent* to represent all the caregivers involved in a child's life.

Send a Letter Describing Morning Meeting

A first step might be to send a letter or email to parents giving them a glimpse of this part of their child's day and describing the learning integral to it. A sample letter is provided below.

Dear Parents,

There's a wonderful beginning to your child's school day! It's called Morning Meeting, and it's a great way to build community, set a positive tone, increase excitement about learning, and improve academic and social skills.

Morning Meeting usually takes between twenty and thirty minutes. First thing each morning, the children and I gather in a circle. We begin by greeting each other. Every day, your child hears their name spoken by a classmate in a friendly and cheerful manner.

Next, students share interesting news with each other in a structured way. Sometimes we go around the circle and all students share; other times a few students share and have a conversation with the class. Sharing helps students listen carefully, think about what they hear, formulate good questions, and learn about each other. During sharing, children have a chance to feel that their ideas are valued and that their classmates care.

After sharing, there is an activity for the whole class. We might sing or recite a poem or play a math game. The activity time helps the class feel united as a group, reinforces academic skills, and helps the children learn how to cooperate and solve problems.

Finally, we read the morning message chart, which helps students think about the day ahead. Sometimes, I use this time to review and practice a reading, punctuation, or math skill.

Every day, Morning Meeting lets children know that school is a safe place where all children's feelings and ideas are important. We'd love to have you visit us for Morning Meeting. Just give me a call to arrange a good time. You'll see for yourself why we're so excited about this start to our day.

Invite Parents to Observe or Participate in Morning Meeting

Often all the explanations about what students are seeing and doing in school and why they're doing it come alive and make more sense when parents experience classroom life for themselves. It can be helpful to post a calendar on the classroom website, with several slots available on each Morning Meeting visiting day. Parents can then sign up for a time that works for them.

Make clear whether you're inviting parents to observe or actively participate in the meeting—or leaving the choice up to them. Some parents feel comfortable participating; others would rather watch first and perhaps participate at a later visit. Either way, knowing what's expected can help make their visit comfortable and productive.

An additional way for parents to observe Morning Meeting—one that might work well for parents who can't come to school during regular school hours—is during an open house. You might try running an adult Morning Meeting that teaches families about Morning Meeting's purpose and structure through the components their children use. By experiencing it for themselves, parents will have a deeper understanding of the benefits of Morning Meeting and will get a taste of the rich learning that happens in meetings every day.

One additional consideration: think about the students in your class and whether or not they'll be comfortable having parents in the classroom. If you think that a parental visit will feel awkward or will interfere with the meeting, consider alternative ways for parents to experience Morning Meeting. For example, you could use technology to offer parents the choice of seeing Morning Meeting without physically being in the classroom.

Share via Communication Channels

With hectic schedules, it may not be possible for parents to experience Morning Meeting first-hand. Consider ways to leverage school-approved communication channels such as private social media pages or communication apps to post videos of Morning Meetings. This not only allows parents a glimpse into the meeting, but provides students the opportunity to view alongside parents and unfold details about their class community.

Understand Morning Meeting Responsibilities

In implementing and assessing Morning Meeting, keep the following general responsibilities in mind.

Teacher's responsibilities:

- Make sure the space is adequate and appropriate for the component. Can a circle be formed? Can all be seen? Can a particular game be safely played?

- Plan a meeting that supports students' academic and social-emotional learning.

- Teach Morning Meeting skills and routines one step at a time, building a scaffold so children can participate successfully in increasingly complex meetings.

- Make necessary accommodations and modifications so that all students can participate.

- Act as timekeeper, keeping things moving.

- Facilitate the meeting, making sure that all class members are greeted, that a variety of students are responding during sharing, and that everyone is participating safely and respectfully in each component.

- Observe students' skills, both social and academic.

- Notice behaviors and reinforce, remind, and redirect using positive language.

- Make sure everyone in the classroom (such as paraprofessionals, visiting parents, or other adults) is included in the meeting if they wish to participate.

Students' responsibilities:

- Get to the meeting promptly and form the circle safely and efficiently.

- Participate fully—contributing actively, listening well, and responding appropriately.

- Interact with a variety of classmates in the friendly spirit of Morning Meeting.

- Move smoothly from Morning Meeting to the next activity.

Common Questions

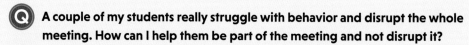 **A couple of my students really struggle with behavior and disrupt the whole meeting. How can I help them be part of the meeting and not disrupt it?**

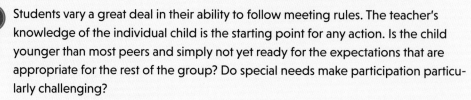 Students vary a great deal in their ability to follow meeting rules. The teacher's knowledge of the individual child is the starting point for any action. Is the child younger than most peers and simply not yet ready for the expectations that are appropriate for the rest of the group? Do special needs make participation particularly challenging?

For the child who is simply too young, a special arrangement about the length of time they attend Morning Meeting makes sense. Give a signal that will let them know when they are to leave the circle, and discuss what they'll do during the remaining meeting time. Gradually, as they are successful with sitting still and paying attention, extend the time they spend in the meeting.

Sometimes a bit of situational assistance is all that is needed. "Miranda, I notice that you have a hard time listening to other people when you sit next to Jin-Ping. You need to pick a different place to sit at Morning Meeting." Or to the fidgeter whose fancy gizmo-watch treats everyone to a rendition of the *Star Wars* theme at least twice in every meeting, "Your watch needs to be in your cubby during Morning Meeting, Gerard."

Some students with lots of overflowing energy are better able to concentrate if they have something that quietly occupies their hands during Morning Meeting. But what about fairness when the rule is to come to the meeting circle empty-handed? This is a complex question about justice that repeats itself with variations all through our lives. In sorting out what to do in each circumstance, we need to consider that fair treatment is responsive to individual needs and doesn't always mean treating people with cookie-cutter sameness. When students trust that their needs, too, will be met in the same spirit of fairness, they are generally able to understand and accept modifications that you make for their classmates.

Sometimes a student's behavior is symptomatic of a need that requires more specialized intervention. A teacher in a fourth/fifth grade inclusion classroom provided a very skillful intervention for a particular student. Andrew was a fifth grader whose special needs manifested in his blurting out inappropriate and rude remarks often unconnected to anything preceding them. This was especially a problem when the class began doing dialogue sharing, in which one person at a time shares information and the rest of the class listens and responds. It became clear that Andrew needed some targeted and intensive instruction so that he could participate in this part of the meeting.

On days when the class did dialogue sharing, Andrew and one of his teachers, Ms. Scamardella (Ms. S), left the circle and moved to a table in the opposite corner of the room where Andrew had "private sharing" with Ms. S while coteacher Ms. Daggett continued the meeting. In his private sharing, Andrew practiced sharing a piece of news appropriately, with no swearing or name-calling. Ms. S modeled careful patterns of suitable responses. Then she shared a piece of news and helped him learn to choose and practice a polite response.

After a few months, Andrew was able to rejoin the group for dialogue sharing, listening quietly most days and, on a really good day, offering a comment or a question "on the spot." In addition, the teachers carefully scheduled Andrew's times to be the sharer so that they could help him plan and rehearse what he would say.

This example illustrates an important point: students' readiness for participation in Morning Meeting can vary widely. They may need a considerable range of modifications or support so they can participate fully in Morning Meeting. If a student is not participating, if their participation is stuck in the negative, or if they are spending more time away from the meeting than in the meeting circle, then clearly the teacher must pay special attention and address the situation, calling on support staff when needed.

Q **I have several children who frequently come in late and a couple who have to leave in the middle of the meeting for special programs. Should they be part of Morning Meeting?**

A Yes, definitely. Morning Meeting is for everyone. Frustrating as the tardiness may be, the meeting time itself is not the time to address it. Latecomers should be greeted pleasantly and welcomed without unduly disrupting whatever is happening in the meeting. To minimize the disruption while still making the latecomer feel welcome, some teachers assign a child the daily job of welcoming latecomers into the circle.

If the lateness is occasional, simply help the child fit into the flow of the day. If it is a chronic problem with a particular child, then some investigation and problem-solving is in order.

In the case of students who have to leave early for "specials," make sure that the greeting can happen with them in the circle, and teach them how to leave the circle quietly and unobtrusively when it is time. If the same students must leave every day, you might think about scheduling a separate time for sharing near the end of the day when everyone can attend.

Q My students are really comfortable with our Morning Meeting, maybe too comfortable. Even I sometimes feel like it's boring. Help!

A A sensitive balance exists between the lovely sense of security that routine can provide and the monotony that can creep in when that routine is unchanging. As students grow comfortable with each other and with the basic format of Morning Meeting, the teacher must act as the "re-balancer" and introduce variation.

This is one reason why retaining the role of meeting planner is so important for teachers, even if they shift some of the meeting responsibilities to students as the year unfolds. Just as in an academic lesson, we need to plan a meeting that will keep students engaged. How can we vary the content and format of each component? How can students interact around meaningful content that is connected to both their interests and the curriculum? Is the content in the meeting too easy or too hard? How much active learning is involved? Are students sitting too long, or are they up and moving during different parts of the meeting?

When teachers consistently consider these questions, purposeful and engaging Morning Meetings result. But if teachers frequently run meetings on the fly, the meetings can quickly become boring and stale.

Q Students in my classroom usually choose to sit next to their friends. Any ideas for making this work better?

A Calling this seating habit to students' attention within the context of the larger purposes of Morning Meeting is often enough intervention. "I notice," says the teacher, "that for the last several mornings, many of us have been choosing to sit next to our good friends. Remember that one of the purposes of Morning Meeting is to help us get to know and feel comfortable with everyone—including those who are not already our friends. Think about that when you choose where you will sit this morning." Tying what may seem a superficial detail to our grander vision helps students see the underlying significance of where we choose to sit and why this choice merits attention.

Sometimes formalizing these expectations and then using verbal cues is necessary. Terms like "new friends day" or "meeting seating" can be useful shorthand for reminding students of expectations, such as to sit next to different people than they sat near yesterday. A note about gender-based seating arrangements: while students may, especially in older grades, tend to group themselves into same-gender clusters, it's best not to dictate a boy-girl seating pattern. Not all students identify in a binary way, and some may feel unwelcome in the circle if such an arrangement is required. There are many inclusive ways to mix up the seating arrangements. For example, have students hold up one finger if their birthday falls on an odd day and two fingers if it falls on an even day, and alternate ones and twos around the circle.

The same can be done with the number of letters in their first name, a preference (ones prefer summer, twos prefer winter), and many other characteristics that can apply to any student.

Teachers can also engineer different mixes that shake up entrenched patterns. In some primary classes, students make and decorate "sit-upons" with their names. Teachers then use these cushions to assign seats, rotating placement often so that children sit next to many class members. In older classes, a round of Baseball greeting, the Skip greeting, or a Warm Wind Blows (pages 60, 72, and 136) will shake up the seating arrangement.

Sometimes students themselves will notice a problem—and will have great ideas for addressing it. One winter morning when a group of fourth grade students were called to Morning Meeting, a student raised his hand. "Mrs. Davis," he said, "everyone always sits next to the same person each day in Morning Meeting." Around the circle, his classmates nodded in agreement. Later that day during closing circle, the class decided to create a list of patterns they could use to arrange themselves in Morning Meeting. It was an extremely long list including ideas such as ABC order according to first, middle, or last name; numerical order according to their house or apartment number; birthday order; alternating color of eyes (blue, brown, green); sit next to a new person every day; sit next to someone from a different table; and so on. The class decided to post a different seating order each day on the morning message to guide how students arranged themselves in the circle. However, the teacher made sure that a couple of days each week were free-choice seating days because the ultimate goal was to have them choose to meet and interact with a variety of people.

 In my classroom, there is a child nobody wants to sit next to. How should I address this?

 It is not uncommon for students to deliberately ostracize a certain child by not sitting next to them. Action is required on two fronts—one immediate, the other longer term.

First, do whatever you must to stop the exclusion-by-seating. Remove the element of choice by assigning rotating seating patterns (see previous question). Or assign partners who will sit together at Morning Meeting and work together during any partner activities within the meeting.

The longer-term solution begins with observing and reflecting on why this child is not accepted. Is this an instance of bullying or prebullying behavior? Or is some other dynamic at play? Is a specific group of students doing the excluding? Or is this a whole-class problem?

If specific children seem to lead the exclusionary actions, you could set up a time to talk with them, both to understand more about what's going on and to make clear that this is not acceptable behavior. If it's a whole-class problem, you could schedule a class meeting at a separate time from Morning Meeting. However, you'll need to carefully structure the discussion in a way that protects the child who has been ostracized. One way to do this is to read and discuss a book chosen for its relevant plot, which allows the discussion of the social issue to happen at a slight remove from actual classroom circumstances.

Q **What is the difference between a class meeting and Morning Meeting?**

A Class meetings are held for the purpose of solving a problem, or perhaps planning for a project or event or debriefing afterward. They are generally not held every day.

Morning Meeting is held for the purposes named earlier in the chapter and is held every day. It is not used as a time to solve problems or take care of general classroom business. Teachers who use both kinds of meetings often comment that many of the habits of participation and social skills that are developed through Morning Meeting help students succeed with democratic, cooperative processes like class meetings.

Q **I have students in my class from diverse cultural backgrounds. Are there special things I should keep in mind when planning Morning Meetings?**

A Since the heart of Morning Meeting is creating spaces where each child is a valued member of the community, it's important to spend some time learning about the students you teach. Understanding unique, diverse backgrounds will provide an understanding of the particular challenges each child might face and the strengths each might bring. Although it's best to learn from the students and their families, some time spent in the library or on the internet is also worthwhile. Here are some questions to ask:

- What are the traditions for greeting people in the student's culture?

- What has the student probably learned about how to behave toward adults? Toward peers? Toward peers of the same gender? Of a different gender?

- Is it culturally acceptable to touch a classmate? Is it culturally acceptable to make eye contact?

- What are the expectations regarding education for boys? For girls?

Knowing the answers to some of these questions will help you plan Morning Meeting structures that will ease the student's transition. For example, if a child is not accustomed to touching other people, a greeting in which children pass a ball or other small object around the circle (see page 59) can help the child begin to feel comfortable with physically interactive greetings. And if you have taken the time to learn about family and cultural customs, you may be able to invite the student to share them through Morning Meeting—for example, by having the class do a greeting using a common greeting phrase from their home culture. This helps the child feel welcomed while enriching the class's learning and appreciation of world cultures.

Q **Morning Meeting runs well when I'm in the classroom, but I'm concerned about what will happen when I'm out and a guest teacher is there. How can I ensure success for both the guest teacher and the students?**

A With some planning on your part, guest teachers can be very successful with Morning Meeting. First, create a standard Morning Meeting plan that can be used when you're absent. Keep it simple but engaging for children. In your notes to the guest teacher, explain the four components and write out directions for each. For the morning message, one idea that works well is to write a standard message on a chart and laminate it so that each time you have a guest teacher, you or the guest teacher can put in the correct date and other customizations with dry-erase markers.

Next, practice this standard Morning Meeting with students prior to having a guest teacher. Be sure students know how to do each of the components, and address any possible snags. You could even invite a colleague to play the role of guest teacher while you are there so you could observe, see where the rough spots might be, and make adjustments.

Greeting

A Friendly and Respectful Salute

"Good morning, Morgan." Hector speaks seriously and earnestly, for that is who Hector is. He looks directly at Morgan, who sits on his left, and offers his right hand.

"Good morning, Hector!" returns Morgan. He grins widely and grasps Hector's hand with exuberance. Morgan's "Good mornings" are always punctuated with invisible exclamation points, for that is who Morgan is.

Shannon, on Morgan's left, shifts a bit and sits up taller, ready to receive the enthusiasm of a greeting, Morgan-style. And here it comes. "Good morning, Shannon!" "Good morning, Morgan!" Her teacher smiles, pleased with Shannon's strong voice. Shannon had entered the third grade classroom in September with a tentative air. In Morning Meeting, her fade-into-the-chair posture and barely audible voice seemed designed to help her escape the notice of her peers. Now, four months and more than seventy Morning Meetings later, here she is, wearing a smile almost as broad as Morgan's, her hand extended and waiting for his.

And so it goes around the circle. In just a few minutes, every member of the circle—children, teacher, assistant teacher, and Matthew's mother, who is visiting this morning—has been greeted by name, with a handshake and a friendly smile.

Overview

Morning Meeting begins with greeting. Each student greets and is greeted by name. This single act sends a powerful message that each and every student is seen and expresses gratitude for their unique presence. Even on days when time doesn't allow for a full Morning Meeting, teachers convene the circle and make sure greeting takes place. It is that important because of the tone it sets and the way that tone carries into the rest of the day.

Some mornings, the greeting is basic and straightforward, as described in the opening vignette. Variations might be simple, such as students tossing a ball to the person whom they are greeting or substituting a high five for the handshake. Other mornings, the greeting process is more elaborate. Some greetings work with all ages; others have features that make them appropriate only for younger grades or complex steps better suited to older students. But no matter how simple or complicated the greeting, all students begin the day hearing their name spoken clearly and making friendly contact with peers.

Purposes and Goals of Greeting

Although the primary purposes of greeting are interpersonal, greetings also offer an opportunity to practice academic skills. For example, in the Skip greeting (page 72), students practice counting or learning about intervals; in the Adjective greeting (page 58), students practice their knowledge of descriptive words. However, we take care to keep the skills being practiced simple and familiar enough that the focus remains on the greeting itself—on seeing and being seen as a significant member of the learning community.

Long or short, dignified or playful, greetings share four common purposes that are explored in the following sections.

Goals of Greeting

- Set a positive tone for the classroom and the day.

- Provide a sense of recognition and belonging.

- Help students learn and use each other's names.

- Give practice in offering hospitality.

Greeting Sets a Positive Tone for the Classroom and the Day

Welcoming, friendly, respectful—these are attributes that characterize the climate in exemplary classrooms. Beginning Morning Meeting with greeting helps create such a climate.

Having a designated greeting each day is important. Though greeting allows plenty of room for individual personality to shine through—Hector's "Good morning" is different from Morgan's, which is different from Shannon's—it also has a structure that provides equity and safety.

The goal in Morning Meeting greeting is for all to greet and be greeted equally. Within a classroom community, starting the day by hearing your name spoken with respect and warmth is not a privilege for just a popular few. It is, instead, a right to which all are entitled. When we make time for greeting every morning, no matter how full the schedule, we send a clear message as teachers that we expect class members to treat each other with courtesy and equity and that we will do our best to make sure that they do so.

Being Greeted Provides a Sense of Recognition and Belonging

Being greeted by name is a very basic way of gaining a sense of recognition and belonging. The student Sue (whom you met in the foreword) went ungreeted and unseen for seven-eighths of her day. Unseen, she felt she was not there. Because she was old enough to do something about it, she chose to physically remove herself. Sadly, our classrooms have too many other children who, though physically present, walk through their days feeling unacknowledged and unseen.

Think of the old expression "neither here nor there," meaning something that is unimportant and irrelevant, the opposite of how we want our students to feel. We want them to feel important, to be "here." And so they must feel seen. The act of intentional greeting is an act of sincere recognition of each child, every day.

Making sure that everyone sees and is seen is an important way to prevent the formation of cliques or other tightly bonded and highly exclusive groups that can cause others to feel left out. Greeting provides opportunities for students to learn how to welcome everyone and form groups with people other than their

Highlights of Greeting

- Ensures that every child names and notices others at the outset of the day and is named in return

- Allows the teacher to observe and take the pulse of the group that day

- Provides practice in elements of effective communication, such as looking at each other, using a friendly voice and friendly body language, speaking clearly and audibly, listening respectfully, and waiting one's turn

- Requires students to extend the range of classmates they spontaneously notice and greet

- Helps students to reach across gender, clique, and friendship lines

- Challenges the intellect (for example, when the greeting structure uses math patterns, phrases in various languages, and set-making) and provides practice in academic skills

closest friends. Looking each other in the eye, smiling, and greeting each other by name—or a self-chosen nickname—is an important and powerful demonstration of respect that is witnessed by the entire group.

Greeting Helps Students Learn and Use One Another's Names

Knowing someone's name and feeling comfortable using it can provide many opportunities for personal connection. We are able to call on others during a discussion, get another person's attention, ask a question, request help, offer congratulations, ask to join in their play at recess, or whisper an apology.

We can't assume that just because students are grouped together they will all learn one another's names. Halfway through the school year, a teacher from a small regional school, where students from several adjacent towns met for the first time in fifth grade, asked a student to hand a set of papers back to the class. He was surprised to find that she couldn't do it. Why? She couldn't match the names on the papers with the faces of her peers. She simply didn't know all her classmates' names.

A student who doesn't know her classmates well enough to hand them their work is unlikely to feel familiar enough with them to offer her dissenting opinion about a character in a short story, or admit that she doesn't quite get this business of "3 is to 21 as x is to 28," or share a poem she wrote about her grandmother. That would be a great loss, for her, for her classmates, and for the classroom community as a whole.

Knowing that others know our name and hearing our name used is also a reminder of our identity, our individuality within a larger whole. Students identify with their school, their class within that school, their athletic teams, and other extracurricular groups they may be part of. They are Pine Street School students, members of the Tigers basketball team, choir singers, or 4-H club members. While we value feeling like a part of larger communities, it's also essential to retain our sense of individuality. Hearing our name lets us know that someone cares about speaking to us as an individual and recognizes the importance of our perspectives and opinions. Being greeted by name builds connection between classmates and builds confidence in each individual's contribution to the group.

Greeting Provides Practice in Offering Hospitality

Educator and author Parker Palmer writes, "Hospitality is always an act that benefits the host even more than the guest. The concept of hospitality arose in ancient times when this reciprocity was easier to see: In nomadic cultures, the food and shelter one gave to a stranger yesterday is the food and shelter one hopes to receive from a stranger tomorrow. By offering hospitality, one participates in the endless reweaving of a social fabric on which all can depend" (Palmer 2007, 50).

Welcoming each other to our classroom every day is an act of hospitality. The offering of that welcome, one to another, affirms that we are caretakers of each other in that community. Being a host also implies, builds, and strengthens a person's ownership and investment in that place.

We practice daily the skills of welcoming each other—the clear voice, the friendly smile, the careful remembering that Nicholas likes to be called Nick, the firm handshake. When guests visit and are part of our circle, we extend a welcome to them as well, although it can feel a bit awkward at first. "Should we call him Mike or Mr. DiAngelo?" whispers Andy to his teacher when he notices that his friend Matt's father is coming to Morning Meeting. "Could you check with him and see which would feel more comfortable?" replies his teacher.

Several important messages are conveyed in this suggestion. First, our culture offers no single right answer to the question of how to address elders. Some parents prefer being called by their first names; others deem it disrespectful. Second, the role of a host is to make the guest feel respected and comfortable. And third, asking a polite and direct question is a fine way to get an answer you need. It is practice in assertiveness seasoned with courtesy, not an easy blend to achieve at any age.

Kindergarten teacher Eileen Mariani related the story of a January morning in her room: the habit of greeting within the Morning Meeting circle had been well established. On that particular morning, it was Isaac's turn to begin the greeting. Isaac was a shy boy who approached this task with some trepidation. Eileen watched carefully, ready to help if Isaac seemed worried at any point. But, no need, he was doing splendidly.

"Good Morning, Friends" (page 67) was the greeting, and it had been clapped and stamped with a nicely modulated glee around the circle, just returning to Isaac, when he glanced up and then stood abruptly, heading for the door. Eileen, whose view of the door was blocked by a bookshelf, also rose to see what was going on. There stood Isaac, framed by the doorway, hand extended to a distinguished-looking visitor who was entering the room with the principal. "Good morning, Mr. . . . uh . . . I'm sorry, what is your name, please?" Isaac proceeded to shake the visitor's hand before walking gravely back to his place on the rug to continue the meeting.

The months of modeling and practicing, the discussions of "What can you do if you don't remember someone's name?" had taken hold and enabled Isaac to extend graceful hospitality and true welcome, not just during Morning Meeting with classmates, but beyond it, even to a guest at the door.

Getting Started

Browse the Greeting Ideas section on page 57 as you get started!

As you introduce this component to students and plan the greetings you will use, consider the following guidance.

Pay Attention to How You Introduce Greeting

"Every morning, we're going to greet each other in a friendly and respectful way," a third grade teacher says as she introduces greeting to students. With this simple sentence, she has noted and named two elements of successful greetings. She doesn't stop there—she follows up with discussion, modeling, and practice to make sure that students understand what a friendly and respectful greeting looks and sounds like. But those first words used to introduce greeting establish basic expectations from the outset.

It's important to clarify that you don't expect students to be best friends with everyone in the class, but you do expect them to be friendly and to treat everyone with respect. Then take time to discuss the details. What does it sound like to say "Good morning" with a friendly tone? What does a firm handshake feel like? Paying attention to these details makes a tremendous difference in the success of greeting.

Model and Practice Greeting Routines and Procedures

Even in the most basic "Good morning" greeting, students need to look at their classmate, and, using the classmate's name, say "Good morning" with a friendly tone and a clear voice. That's a lot to remember.

For the greeting to go smoothly and be a positive start to the day, it's important to model and practice common skills. These include:

- Sitting or standing in your own space in the circle
- Speaking in a clear, audible voice
- Using a friendly tone
- Using friendly body language
- Shaking hands safely
- Waiting your turn
- Listening while others greet

 Scan the QR code to see a teacher using Interactive Modeling to set up a successful greeting.

Interactive Modeling (see page 27) is a good strategy to use for teaching greeting skills. You might begin by saying, "Our rules say 'Be kind to each other.' One way to do that is to be sure we greet each other in a friendly way. Watch while I greet John, and notice what I do."

When you ask the class what they noticed during the demonstration, guide them in naming all the important elements: looking at the person being greeted, smiling, using their name, and speaking in a friendly voice.

In the days that follow, and periodically throughout the year, reinforce these and any additional greeting skills the class learns. For example: "What did you notice about the way we did our greeting today?" "What makes it easier to speak loudly and clearly?"

Keep Greetings Simple at First and Build Complexity Over Time

When first introducing greeting, a simple, direct "Good morning, [classmate's name]" works best. When students are able to do that fluently and in a consistently friendly way, introduce other elements, keeping in mind students' ages, skill levels, and experience with Morning Meeting.

Here is one possible progression (be sure to model each element you add):

- Teach a basic "Good morning" greeting (page 67).
- Add an item, such as a ball or soft toy, for students to pass around the circle.
- Add a handshake or other physical contact.
- Add movement, music, or both.
- Add an element of choice (for example, choosing a movement to make, choosing a classmate to greet).

Help Students Learn Each Other's Names

Names are powerful part of personal identity. Before you can help students learn each other's names, it will be important for you to learn each student's name and correct pronunciation. Practice and confirm the correct pronunciation of names one-on-one with students as you welcome them to school.

Name tags are a great help in the early days of school, and many greetings focus on learning names. Starting the year with choral greetings in which everyone says or sings the names together can help everyone feel more comfortable in the process of learning classmates' names, particularly in the younger grades. When children are ready to say names individually, assigning pairs ahead of time so that each person is prepared to say a partner's name can help boost children's confidence.

Older children also benefit from structures that help them learn names. On the first day of school, you might choose to issue a challenge: "Let's see if all of us can learn each other's names by the end of the second week of school." Students are often eager to take up the challenge, and many of them will feel confident that they'll learn names in the first week. At the end of the challenge period, give students a chance to see if they can name everyone in the meeting circle, and watch the smiles as each student hears their name.

Use Opportunities to Practice Academic Skills

In addition to building community and helping students feel welcomed, greeting can be a time for reviewing academic content or practicing academic skills.

For example, a Skip greeting (page 72), which can be adapted for any age group, offers an opportunity to practice math skills. Younger children get to practice counting; older children can take responsibility for calculating the number of "skips" needed to ensure that all are greeted. Or if the class is learning about adjectives, students can each greet their neighbor and add, "I'm having a _____ day so far. What about you?" with each student filling in the blank with an adjective.

In Greeting Ideas (beginning on page 57), you'll find a number of greetings that incorporate academic content or skills practice.

Consider Ways for Students to Take Responsibility for Aspects of Greeting

Although you, as teacher, will want to keep hold of planning and managing Morning Meeting, you can give students responsibility for certain elements of greeting. For example, you might give individuals responsibility for choosing the day's greeting from a short list of familiar greetings. (Be sure to rotate this privilege among all students; also check on their choice ahead of time to make sure it fits the needs of the group on that day.)

Another way to give students responsibility, especially later in the year, is to have them devise new greetings. In one fourth grade class, students collaborated in language arts block to create and write up ideas for new greetings. The teacher worked with them to refine their ideas and then incorporated these greetings into Morning Meeting, asking students to help introduce and model each one.

Anticipate and Help Students Handle Awkward Moments

Norah turns to greet Shane but, in the moment, forgets his name. As a class nears the end of a Ball Toss greeting (page 59), Josiah freezes and then tosses the ball to a student who has already been greeted. Awkward moments happen. Although it's not possible to avoid all such moments, anticipation and planning can diminish their frequency and intensity.

Sometimes the solution is as simple as posing a question before the greeting: "What can we do if we forget someone's name?" During the brief discussion that follows, students conclude that they can nicely ask someone's name. They also suggest that if they see the person greeting them hesitate, they can help out by whispering their name. For greetings that require students to notice and remember who has been greeted, teachers might devise a signal ("Thumbs-up until you're greeted"). Such signals help the last few greeters who may be struggling to remember who remains to be greeted.

As greetings get more complex or higher in risk, you'll need to anticipate potentially hurtful situations. Sometimes students get into a pattern of greeting the most popular classmates first

and leaving the same students, over and over, to be greeted last. If you notice this dynamic occurring, remind students that the purpose of greeting is for all to feel welcomed and part of the group. Then select greetings that encourage students to move out of their friendship groups. For example, you might do a Cross-Circle greeting (page 64) and ask students to greet someone across the circle to whom they haven't spoken that morning.

Understand Greeting Responsibilities

In implementing and assessing greeting, keep the following general responsibilities in mind.

Teacher's responsibilities:

- Teach a variety of age-appropriate greetings.

- Model aspects of a warm and respectful greeting.

- Make sure everyone uses friendly and appropriate words and body language.

- As students are ready, give them responsibility for choosing greetings.

- Teach greeting skills and routines gradually, scaffolding so students can participate successfully in increasingly complex greetings.

Students' responsibilities:

- Vary whom they sit next to.

- Wait for their turn to greet.

- Listen carefully to the other greetings.

- Use a clear, audible voice.

- Use friendly and appropriate body language and tone of voice.

Common Questions

Q **Do I need to do greeting every single day? What about days when we have no time, when the art teacher is waiting to start the art lesson, or we're going on a field trip and need to leave right away?**

A It's important to do greeting every day, but greeting doesn't need to take a lot of time. When time is tight, you could do a greeting like Righty/Lefty (page 71), in which students all turn and greet their neighbors at the same time.

For the "Tuesday-is-art-right-away" situation, when the time crunch will be regular, you might suggest that the art teacher join you for five minutes to be part of the class greeting before beginning the art lesson.

On field trip days, teachers sometimes gather students after reaching their destination for a brief check-in and a simple greeting.

Q **How do I ensure greetings are inclusive?**

A Simple greetings that require only a word—or no words at all—are a good starting point. Greetings like this are low-risk and accessible, allowing students to participate regardless of their social, emotional, cognitive, or verbal skills. Greetings can begin with just a wave and a smile. Then add simple words such as "Hi," "Hello," or "Good morning," followed by learning the pronunciation of classmates' names. Continue to add more complex language as students are ready. As you add more complex greetings to the repertoire, consider providing additional support. For students with limited English proficiency, you might provide a chance to practice the greetings with a partner or small group before using them in Morning Meeting. For students with severe social anxiety who may suddenly freeze up when their turn arrives, even if they have practiced a greeting, provide a nonverbal alternative to all that can be used in these moments.

Additionally, songs and chants are wonderful ways for students to become comfortable with new language forms. Often, phrases that are hard to say fluently are much easier to use when set to music.

We can also be inclusive by being in tune with cultural perspectives. Keep in mind that every culture has its own way of greeting people and that students from some cultures might feel a tension between classroom greetings and what they are accustomed to. For example, some students have been taught at home to avoid eye contact with each other or, more often, with adults as an indication of respect. In some countries, hugging or shaking hands is a gesture of friendship. In other countries, it's not culturally acceptable to touch other people. In yet other countries, cross-gender handshakes are taboo, whereas same-gender friends greet each other with a kiss. This is where it pays to do a little research into students' home cultures.

Another idea is to have all students learn to greet each other in the home languages of students who are English language learners. This can help these students feel more welcome, and it can give native English speakers an opportunity to gain some insight into the difficulties of functioning in a new language.

Finally, consider providing visual supports, which you can post on or near the morning message. These can include the words of the greeting neatly written out along with drawings or photographs of any accompanying movements.

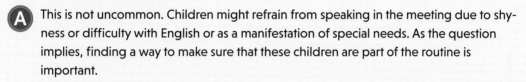

What about the child who just doesn't speak in front of the group? How can I help them participate in greeting?

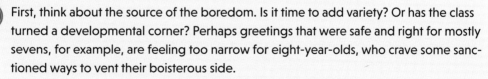

This is not uncommon. Children might refrain from speaking in the meeting due to shyness or difficulty with English or as a manifestation of special needs. As the question implies, finding a way to make sure that these children are part of the routine is important.

Something that often helps is practicing with the child individually before the meeting and making sure that they know whom they will greet. Kindergarten teacher Elisabeth Olivera, who teaches in a bilingual classroom, suggests that the teacher and student say the words together, with the teacher gradually softening their voice until the child is comfortable speaking on their own.

You can also help the group understand what is going on and how they can be encouraging. The explanation should be simple and matter-of-fact. For the young and reluctant speaker, you might say, "Terry doesn't want to talk in Morning Meeting yet, but I hope that he will soon. Until he does, you can help by making sure he is greeted, and I will help by greeting the next person with him."

This is a wonderful opportunity to validate that we all have different comfort levels with different activities and that we can help one another by being accepting and encouraging.

Students seem to be getting bored with greeting. What can I do?

First, think about the source of the boredom. Is it time to add variety? Or has the class turned a developmental corner? Perhaps greetings that were safe and right for mostly sevens, for example, are feeling too narrow for eight-year-olds, who crave some sanctioned ways to vent their boisterous side.

To add variety, take a look at the week as a whole and then find ways to vary the greetings day-to-day. For example, one day pass a greeting around the circle, another day do a group chant as a greeting, and another day do a greeting that involves movement or one where students get to choose whom to greet. Keeping a log of the different greetings you use can help you notice patterns and increase the variety of greetings you use.

Besides introducing new greetings, you can work with students to come up with adaptations of old favorites. For example, a group of fifth graders at Kensington Avenue Elementary School (now Kensington International School) in Springfield, Massachusetts, invented the Elbow Rock greeting (page 66) in which they extend

, bent at the elbow, and shake arms rather than hands.

Q **I teach in the upper grades and students usually start out fine with greeting. However, as the year goes on, they tend to get sloppy and silly. They complain that greeting is babyish and that they know everyone's names and don't see why they have to keep doing this.**

A This is not an unusual occurrence, particularly with older students as they get used to Morning Meeting, comfortable with the class, and lax with expectations. When you see behaviors such as whispering, nudging, in-jokes, fake smiles, and muttered names, it's time to stop the meeting. These kinds of behaviors are a signal that the class has lost sight of the real purpose behind greeting and needs some help to get back on track.

Review the goals and purposes of greeting. Remind the group that greetings welcome and acknowledge people in the classroom community and that this is important work. Sometimes sharing a story with students, such as the one offered earlier about Sue (who never felt acknowledged) or the story of a time when you, as an adult, felt unnoticed, helps to remind children of the importance of what they are doing. A discussion about how a sincere versus an insincere greeting really feels may also be helpful. You might ask students for suggestions of ways to make greeting work better while also holding them to the expectation that they greet each other in a respectful and friendly way.

Also, think about the greetings you've been using. Are some getting too familiar? Consider trying some new types of greetings to keep things fresh.

Greeting Ideas

On the following pages, you'll find some ideas of greetings to try with your class. The chart below can help you start thinking about which greetings will work best for the students you teach, and whether to introduce a greeting at the beginning of the year when students are still getting to know one another or a little bit later in the year. As always, defer to your own knowledge of the children in your class to determine the best choices.

Group Activity for:

 Beginning of Year

 Later in Year

 Younger Grades

 Older Grades

 Academic Content Reinforcement

 Songs, Chants, and Movements

Greeting	PAGE	Beginning of Year	Later in Year	Younger Grades	Older Grades	Academic Content Reinforcement	Songs, Chants, and Movements
Adjective	58		✓	✓	✓	✓	
Albert Einstein	58		✓		✓	✓	✓
Ball Toss	59	✓		✓	✓		✓
Baseball	60		✓	✓	✓		✓
Book Character	60		✓	✓	✓		
Cheer	61		✓		✓		✓
Cheering Section	62	✓	✓	✓	✓		
Come to the Circle if . . . Mathematician-Style	63		✓		✓	✓	
Cross-Circle	64	✓		✓	✓		
Dice	64		✓		✓	✓	
Different Languages	65	✓		✓	✓	✓	
Double Takes	66		✓		✓		
Elbow Rock	66		✓		✓		
"Good Morning"	67	✓	✓	✓	✓		
"Good Morning, Friends"	67		✓	✓			✓
"Hello, Neighbor"	68		✓	✓			✓
Interview	68	✓		✓	✓		
Knock, Knock	69	✓		✓			
Marbles	69		✓	✓	✓		
Math Match Card	70		✓		✓	✓	✓
Name Card	70	✓		✓	✓		
One-Minute	70		✓	✓	✓		
One, Two, Three, Four	71		✓		✓		✓
Pantomime	71	✓		✓	✓		
Righty/Lefty	71		✓	✓	✓		
Sawubona-Sikhona	72		✓		✓		
Science Friction	72	✓		✓		✓	
Skip	72		✓		✓	✓	
Snowball	73		✓	✓	✓		
Spiderweb	73		✓	✓	✓		
What's Your Place Value?	73		✓	✓	✓	✓	

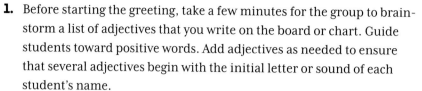

Adjective

Group Activity for:

 Beginning of Year

Later in Year

Younger Grades

Older Grades

Academic Content Reinforcement

 Songs, Chants, and Movements

1. Before starting the greeting, take a few minutes for the group to brainstorm a list of adjectives that you write on the board or chart. Guide students toward positive words. Add adjectives as needed to ensure that several adjectives begin with the initial letter or sound of each student's name.

2. Each student chooses an adjective that begins with the same sound as their first name.

3. Going around the circle, students introduce themselves by saying, "Hello, my name is [adjective] [first name]." For example: "Hello, my name is Jazzy Janet!"

4. Classmates respond, "Hello, Jazzy Janet!"

Variation: If there's time, students often like the challenge of going around the circle a second time and trying to name each classmate using the classmate's chosen adjective.

Albert Einstein

1. In advance, find quotations by Albert Einstein (or other famous scientists) to inspire students or relate to their science learning. For example: "The important thing is not to stop questioning. Curiosity has its own reason for existence."

2. Give each student a slip of paper or index card with a different quotation on it.

3. Have students mix and mingle to greet each other and take turns reading their quotation and briefly sharing what it means to them.

4. Have students greet as many classmates as time permits.

Ball Toss

1. A child begins by greeting another child and then gently throwing, rolling, or bouncing a ball to them. If you're using a small, soft ball, throwing underhand works best. Roll or softly bounce a large, bouncy ball.

2. The second child returns the greeting (but not the ball) and chooses a new classmate to greet and pass the ball to.

3. Continue in this way until all have been greeted once. The greeting ends when the ball returns to the starter.

Variations: Make this greeting more challenging and build cooperation among older students in one of the following ways:

- Pass the greeting ball around the circle as explained above. Now students pass the ball around one more time silently (with no greeting or talking), repeating the pattern the ball just made. Students will enjoy passing the ball several times this way and competing against the clock.

- Pass the greeting ball as explained above. Repeat, passing the ball silently in the same pattern, and as the ball goes around, add one or two more balls at even intervals so that several balls are being passed in the original greeting pattern. Challenge students to see if they can pass the balls around three times without dropping them or skipping anyone. You can also add the element of competition against the clock.

- Once the greeting ball has gone around the first time, have students "undo the greeting pattern" by sending the ball in the reverse direction while saying, "Have a good day!" or some other encouraging words.

Baseball

1. Explain and post the following definitions: single = one base; double = two bases; triple = three bases; home run = four bases. Before the greeting, agree on a signal that indicates, "I've been greeted!" such as crossed arms or a thumbs-up.

2. All students stand; choose one to be the first batter.

3. The batter decides what type of hit they've made (for example, a triple) and begins to walk around the inside of the circle.

4. Each student they pass represents a base. As they pass first base and second base, they high-five these students.

5. When they reach third base, they say, "Good morning, [classmate's name]," to the student there, who returns the greeting.

6. The batter takes the greeted student's place in the circle and gives the signal that indicates they've been greeted.

7. The greeted student becomes the next batter and the process continues, with students skipping anyone who's already been greeted, until everyone has been greeted.

Book Character

1. This greeting can be used with any number of greeting structures. For a week, students wear name tags of their favorite book character and greet each other using characters' names.

2. At the end of the week, have students remove their name tags and see if they can remember one another's character names.

Group Activity for:

  Beginning of Year

 Later in Year

 Younger Grades

 Older Grades

 Academic Content Reinforcement

Songs, Chants, and Movements

Cheer

Going around the circle, students do the following call-and-response greeting:

Student: My name is [first name].
Group: YEAH!
Student: And I like to [activity].
Group: Uh-huh.
Student: And I'll be a [person who does this activity].
Group: YEAH!
Student: Every day of my life.
Group: Every day of their life.

For example:
Student: My name is Carla.
Group: YEAH!
Student: And I like to swim.
Group: Uh-huh.
Student: And I'll be a swimmer.
Group: YEAH!
Student: Every day of my life.
Group: Every day of her life.

Cheering Section

This greeting can be used the day of a test or assessment.

1. Everyone starts by holding their thumb up.

2. Students choose whom to greet and give them a cheer for the day.

3. The person who is greeted says "Thank you," and then puts their thumb down. Then, they choose a person whose thumb is still up to cheer on.

4. The last student cheers the teacher on to end the greeting.

> For example:
> Cory: Good morning, Kristen! Be persistent!
> Kristen: Thank you, Cory! Good morning, Kerry. You got this!

Variations:

- Greet students going around the circle instead of letting them choose with thumbs up.

- Have all students start standing and sit as they have been greeted, or vice versa.

- Brainstorm a list of encouraging phrases to use in the greeting. Options include:

  - You got this!

  - Take your time!

  - You can do it!

  - Good luck!

  - No worries!

  - Do your best!

  - Be persistent!

  - We believe in you!

Group Activity for:

  Beginning of Year

Later in Year

 Younger Grades

 Older Grades

 Academic Content Reinforcement

 Songs, Chants, and Movements

Come to the Circle if . . . Mathematician-Style

1. Before coming to the circle, each student receives an index card with a prewritten fraction. Prompt students to look at their own cards and think, "Is my fraction less than one whole? Is it greater than one whole? Greater or less than ½? Is it equal to ½?"

2. Have students turn and talk to a partner to share their ideas about their fraction.

3. Invite students to the circle to greet each other based on the characteristics of their fraction. Say, "Come to the circle if your fraction is ___." Fill in the blank with different categories.

4. When the students come to the circle, they can greet each other in any familiar way you have chosen (for example, handshake, fist bump, wave, etc.).

5. After greeting, students go back to their seats, and you call the next category.

6. Continue until all students have been in the center for the greeting.

Variation: You can use any grade-level mathematics content for this greeting. Consider expanding to other content areas as well; you could include vocabulary words, historical events, and more!

Cross-Circle

1. Before the greeting, agree on a signal that indicates, "I've been greeted!"

2. The first student greets someone sitting on the other side of the circle, who returns the greeting and gives the "I've been greeted" signal.

3. That person greets someone else who is across the circle from them, and so on until everyone has been greeted.

Variation: Choose a specific theme, such as cross-circle someone-wearing-the-same-color-as-you greeting, cross-circle someone-you-haven't-spoken-to-yet-this-morning greeting, and so on.

Group Activity for:

 Beginning of Year

 Later in Year

 Younger Grades

 Older Grades

 Academic Content Reinforcement

 Songs, Chants, and Movements

Dice

1. Students sit in the circle. The first student rolls a pair of dice and says a math fact about the numbers rolled. For example, if they roll a six and a five, they could say, "Good morning! Six times five equals thirty."

2. The rest of the class returns the greeting and repeats the math fact.

3. The first greeter now hands the dice to the person on their left, and the greeting continues around the circle.

Variation: Challenge students not to repeat any facts. If they get stuck, let them roll the dice again to get a different combination.

Different Languages for Greeting

Students greet each other in a language other than English. The use of different languages for greeting can be incorporated into many greeting structures. Look up these greetings online to find the correct pronunciation prior to Morning Meeting. You can also look up greetings in other languages related to content the class is studying.

Language	Greeting	Meaning
American Sign Language	Signing "hello" is similar to saluting: with the fingers squeezed together and the palm facing outward, touch the tips of the fingers to the forehead and then move the hand forward	Hello
Arabic	Marhaban	Welcome/Hello
French	Bonjour	Hello/Good morning
German	Guten morgen	Good morning
Greek	Kali mera	Good morning
Haitian Creole	Bonjou	Good morning
Hebrew	Shalom	Hello
Hindi	Namaste	Hello
Italian	Buon giorno	Good morning
Japanese	Konnichiwa	Hello/Good day
Mandarin	Ni hao	Hello
Polish	Dzień dobry	Good day
Russian	Dobroye utro	Good morning
Spanish	Buenos días	Good morning
Swahili	Jambo	Hello
Vietnamese	Xin chào	Hello

Group Activity for:

 Beginning of Year

 Later in Year

 Younger Grades

 Older Grades

 Academic Content Reinforcement

 Songs, Chants, and Movements

 ## Double Takes

1. Before the greeting begins, discuss with students the importance of greeting different people, not just their best friends, and guide them in thinking of strategies for helping each other do this. Also, help them think about the kinds of things they might have in common (hobbies, favorite music or TV shows, sports, etc.). If you think it might be difficult for students to find common interests, you could make the task more specific; for example, ask them to share one thing they each enjoyed about a recent field trip or a favorite song from the school band performance.

2. Students mix and mingle to music, greeting each other with a friendly handshake and a "Good morning, [classmate's name]."

3. When the music stops, students who are greeting each other form pairs and find one thing they have in common—their "double take."

4. After thirty seconds to a minute, invite a few pairs to share their double takes with the class. Repeat as time allows, being sure to have different students share out each time.

 ## Elbow Rock

1. Before the greeting, model and practice doing an "elbow shake": instead of shaking hands, students lock elbows and shake arms.

2. The greeting goes around the circle with each student saying "Good morning" to the next and doing an elbow shake.

 Scan the QR code
to see the Elbow Rock greeting in action.

"Good Morning"

In this basic greeting, two students face each other, smile, and say, "Good morning, [classmate's name]."

Variation: Early in the year, try having students greet each other with a wave, salute, or bow. After a few weeks, when students are more comfortable with each other and with the format of Morning Meeting, you might have students greet each other with:

- A handshake

- A handshake that students make up

- A high five

- A high five and ankle shake

Variation: Going around the circle, students pass a prop that's associated with an academic subject and greet each other using an appropriate title. For example, students might pass a magnifying glass and say, "Good morning, scientist [classmate's name]," or pass a book and say, "Good morning, reader [classmate's name]." Choose props that reinforce an academic focus for the day.

"Good Morning, Friends"

The following chant is a good way to begin the greeting portion of Morning Meeting, to be followed by another structure that allows everyone to be greeted by name, such as saying "Good morning, [classmate's name]" around the circle:

> Good morning, friends.
> Two words so nice to say.
> So clap your hands,
> And stamp your feet,
> And let's start together this way.

Group Activity for:

 Beginning of Year

 Later in Year

 Younger Grades

 Older Grades

 Academic Content Reinforcement

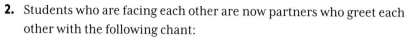 Songs, Chants, and Movements

"Hello, Neighbor"

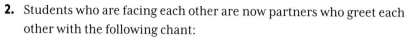

1. Students form an inner and an outer circle, with the inner circle facing the outer circle.

2. Students who are facing each other are now partners who greet each other with the following chant:

> Hello, neighbor, what d'ya say? (Wave to your partner.)
> It's gonna be a wonderful day. (Circle arms over head and then move down to the sides.)
> So clap your hands and boogie on down. (Clap hands and wiggle down.)
> Give a little jump and turn around. (Jump up and turn in place.)

3. The inner circle then moves one person to the right so that everyone has a new partner and repeats the chant. This continues until everyone is back in their original places.

Variation: Instead of jumping, students can raise their hands high ("Then raise your hands and turn around") or, later on when students are more comfortable with physical contact, bumping hips ("Give a little bump and turn around").

Interview

1. On the morning message, ask students to pair up and interview each other. Provide a structure for this interview. For example, you could give students fill-in-the-blank sentences to complete or list two or three questions they can ask.

2. During the meeting, partners introduce each other to the group: "Hi, this is Jimmy. After school, he likes to go roller-skating, and his favorite food is ice cream."

Knock, Knock

Use this variation of an old favorite to have children greet each other and learn last names.

1. The first greeter turns to the student on their left (the receiver), smiles, and pretends to knock on a door:

Greeter:	Knock, knock!
Receiver:	Who's there?
Greeter:	Maya.
Receiver:	Maya who?
Greeter:	Maya Gonzalez!
Whole class:	Good morning, Maya Gonzalez!

2. The receiver becomes the next greeter. Go around the circle until everyone has been greeted.

Marbles

1. Give each student three marbles (or other small objects). Make sure students have a way to distinguish their original marbles from the marbles they receive from other greeters. For example, students could hold their original marbles in their right hand. Alternatively, you could have each student write their name on three cards and use those instead of marbles.

2. When you say, "Go," students mingle, greeting each other by saying, "Good morning, [classmate's name]." Every third person a student greets gets a marble.

3. When a student has given away all three original marbles, they sit down.

Group Activity for:

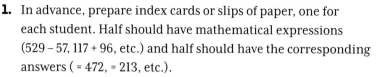

Beginning of Year

Later in Year

Younger Grades

Older Grades

Academic Content Reinforcement

Songs, Chants, and Movements

Math Match Card

1. In advance, prepare index cards or slips of paper, one for each student. Half should have mathematical expressions (529 – 57, 117 + 96, etc.) and half should have the corresponding answers (= 472, = 213, etc.).

2. Give each student a card.

3. Students mix and mingle, looking for the match to their card.

4. Matched students give each other a friendly greeting and sit down so that their equation is visible to the rest of the circle. (The student with the mathematical expression sits to the right of the student with the corresponding answer.)

5. Once everyone has been matched, go around the circle and have each matched pair announce their equation while holding their cards up.

Name Card

1. In advance, write each student's name on a card and shuffle the cards.

2. Place name cards upside down in a stack in the center of the circle.

3. Turn over the top card. The student whose name is on that card begins the greeting.

4. The student gets up and turns over the next card in the stack and greets the child whose name is on that card, then takes that child's place in the circle.

5. The child who has just been greeted turns over the next card, and so on.

6. When all the cards have been used, the greeting ends with the last child greeting the first child.

One-Minute

This is a great greeting to use when time is limited. Students mix and mingle and say, "Good morning, [classmate's name]," to as many other students as they can in one minute. So that the pace doesn't get too frantic, emphasize the importance of standing still and looking at each other with a friendly smile when greeting someone.

One, Two, Three, Four

1. Before beginning, let students know whose name will be called first and in which direction you will go around the circle from there.

2. As a group, the class sings or chants this greeting:

> One, two, three, four,
> Come on, [classmate's name], hit the floor.
> We're so glad you're here today.
> Hurray, hurray, hurray!

3. When a student's name is called, they come into the circle and do whatever they want as a movement (for example, a bow, curtsy, wave, dance, or wiggle) while the rest of the class finishes the song.

4. As the class sings the last line, the student moves back to their place in the circle.

5. Everyone sings the greeting again with the next student's name. This process is repeated around the circle.

Pantomime

1. One student begins by pantomiming something about themselves (favorite activity, food, sport, etc.).

2. The whole class greets them by saying, "Hello, [classmate's name]," and mimicking the pantomime.

3. Continue around the circle until all class members have been greeted.

Righty/Lefty

When you're pressed for time, this quick greeting can come in handy. The one important rule is that students have to look at the person they're greeting to ensure that everyone will feel welcomed and acknowledged.

1. Every other student turns and faces the person to their left, with the remaining students facing right so that everyone has a partner.

2. All at the same time, the people in each pair take turns saying "Good morning, [classmate's name]" to each other.

3. Everyone turns and faces the other direction so that they are now paired with the person sitting on their other side and repeats the greeting.

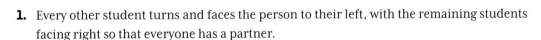

Sawubona-Sikhona

This greeting uses two Zulu phrases: "Sawubona," which means "I see you," and "Sikhona," which means "I am here."

1. All members of the circle close their eyes.

2. One person begins by opening their eyes, turning to the next person, and saying, "Good morning, [neighbor's first name]."

3. That student opens their eyes and responds, "Good morning, [greeter's first name]."

4. The first student then says "Sawubona" to the second student, who responds with "Sikhona." The greeting continues around the circle until all have been greeted.

Group Activity for:

 Beginning of Year

 Later in Year

 Younger Grades

 Older Grades

 Academic Content Reinforcement

Songs, Chants, and Movements

Science Friction

1. Assign partners or have students find a partner.

2. The pairs of students touch their palms together gently and greet each other.

3. Each student rubs their hands vigorously against their own clothes for ten seconds.

4. Again, pairs touch their palms together and greet each other.

5. Afterward, ask students for a quick reflection on what they noticed about any differences between the two greetings.

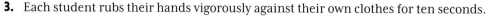

Skip

1. Before the greeting begins, you may want to work with the class to figure out how many spaces to skip to ensure that everyone will be greeted.

2. A student begins by announcing the number of spaces that everyone will skip. For example, they say, "Skip four," walk around the circle to the fifth person, and greet them.

3. The greeter then takes that person's place and sits down.

4. The student who was greeted walks around the circle to the fifth person, greets, switches places, and sits down—and so on until everyone has been greeted. The greeting will flow around the circle several times.

5. The last greeter (the last student standing) greets the whole class, which chorally greets them back.

Snowball

1. Each student writes their name on a sheet of paper, crumples it up so that it looks like a snowball, and tosses it into the center of the circle.

2. Everyone picks up a snowball that landed near them and opens it.

3. One student begins the greeting by walking over to the student whose name is on their snowball and saying, "Good morning, [classmate's name]." The greeter then returns to their place in the circle.

4. The greeted student finds the person whose name is on their own snowball, greets that student, and so on until everyone has been greeted.

Variation: After the initial round of greetings, students recrumple the papers they're holding and toss them. Each student picks up a new snowball, reads the name, and then respectfully observes that student for the rest of the day with a goal of noticing something positive about the student. During a closing circle or end-of-day meeting, students pay a compliment to the classmate they observed.

Spiderweb

1. The student who begins the greeting holds a ball of yarn. They greet someone across the circle and gently roll or toss the ball to that person while firmly holding on to the end of the yarn.

2. The person who receives the ball of yarn greets another student across the circle and sends the ball to that student, making sure to hold on to the unraveling strand with one hand. This continues until everyone has been greeted and the yarn has created a web across the circle.

3. To undo the web, students greet each other in reverse order until the ball of yarn is wound up again.

What's Your Place Value?

This greeting gives students practice with place values but can easily be adapted for other math concepts and skills.

1. Give each student an index card or slip of paper with a three- or four-digit number on it.

2. Choose a number (from zero through nine) and say, for example, "Anyone who has a four in the hundreds place, come to the center to meet and greet."

3. Students who fit that description come to the center of the circle, greet each other with a friendly handshake and a "Good morning, [classmate's name]," and return to their spots in the circle. Repeat until all students have been greeted in at least one round.

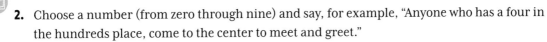

Sharing

The Art and Skill of Conversation

Mr. DiFranco has noticed that students have been choosing the same classmates over and over for all kinds of activities. To help these fourth graders stretch their social circles, he has planned a partner sharing for Morning Meeting, pairing students with classmates they don't usually work or play with. "Today we're going to chat with our partners and find two things that we have in common," he instructs. "At the end, we'll share those things with the class."

Before they begin, he has students generate useful questions they might ask: What do you like to do after school? What kind of movies do you like? What do you like on your pizza? He writes the suggestions on a chart before announcing, "Okay. You'll have two minutes to discover at least two things you have in common and then one more minute to pick which one you will each share with the class."

After a few minutes of lively conversation, students report back to the group. "My partner was Hollis, and we discovered that we both hate anchovies on pizza but we like pepperoni," says Hugo. "And," adds Hollis, "we both have younger brothers." Next, it is Nora's turn. "My partner was Aiden," she begins. "We both like roller coasters!" Aiden continues, "And we both like dogs."

Overview

Sharing follows greeting in Morning Meeting. During sharing, students present news or information about themselves or a topic related to their studies, and classmates respond. There are three main categories of sharing:

- **Around-the-Circle Sharing**—Everyone in the group has an opportunity to briefly share.

- **Partner Sharing**—Students pair up to have a short conversation.

- **Dialogue Sharing**—A few students share, one by one, and the rest of the class responds with questions and comments.

Any of these types of sharing can be focused on a social or academic topic chosen by the teacher. In dialogue sharing, when the topic is chosen for students, it is called *focused topic dialogue sharing*. When it is left open, with students choosing their own topics for sharing, it is called *open-topic dialogue sharing*.

Purposes and Goals of Sharing

Daily sharing helps students get to know each other and plays an important role in building a positive classroom community. Sharing also offers opportunities to reinforce content and skills crucial to success in school and life. When the topic is drawn from academic content, students are getting a content review. And no matter whether the topic is academic or social, students are learning and practicing the critical skills of clear, respectful, caring, empathetic communication, whether they're presenting ideas, formulating relevant questions and comments, or responding to questions and comments.

Whatever the topic, sharing has four common purposes that are explored in the following sections.

Goals of Sharing

- Help students to know each other.

- Develop important social and emotional competencies.

- Teach thinking, listening, and speaking skills.

- Strengthen language development and reading success.

Sharing Helps Students Get to Know One Another

Whereas greeting helps everyone learn and practice the names of class members, sharing takes the next step of helping students know the people attached to the names. Through sharing, we learn about each other—who is proud to be a goalie on their soccer team, who just adopted a rescue dog, who loves graphic novels.

This is true even when everyone responds to the same teacher-chosen topic. "Today we'll have partner chats about something interesting we learned from the biographies we're reading," a teacher might instruct. On another day the teacher might announce, "Our sharing will be an around-the-circle sharing about something you're looking forward to this week." As students respond to these prompts, they reveal unique and individual information.

Often, these revelations help students establish a common ground that is carried beyond the meeting, especially if we help children make and extend connections. "We don't have time for more comments right now, but maybe the three of you could have lunch together and talk more about your favorite sports teams," a teacher might suggest. Or when lots of students seem to agree with statements made in an around-the-circle sharing, a teacher might ask, "When would be a good time to talk more about your connections?"

This kind of gentle guidance helps students move beyond their existing circle of friends. Left to their own devices, they, like all people, tend to spend time with those with whom they're most comfortable, which limits their growth. Sharing allows students to begin with a common interest, a starting place from which to learn about differences as well as similarities. Sharing stretches their understandings of others and encourages consideration of perspectives they might not otherwise have contemplated.

Sharing Develops Important Social and Emotional Competencies

As discussed in Chapter 1, developing certain key social and emotional skills is critical to students' success both in and out of school. Sharing helps build skills in all of these areas.

For example, as Melanie stands to speak during an open-topic sharing, she practices self-awareness. "My dad and I are going camping this weekend, just the two of us. We're going to go fishing, which is something we really love to do!" This upcoming trip is what is most important to Melanie right now. At other times, she might have chosen to share about her interest in ice skating or a movie she had just seen. When the day's sharing topic is open, students learn about the process of choosing a topic. They use self-awareness as they reflect on their interests and values.

Self-awareness also comes into play when students respond to a teacher-chosen topic. For example, Salome's teacher says the topic of the day's sharing is "someone who shows courage." Now Salome has to decide: Will she share about her seventy-two-year-old grandmother, always terrified of the water, who is bravely taking beginner's swimming lessons? Or will she share a story she saw on the evening news about firefighters who rescued three people from an apartment fire?

Students also need to make decisions about the appropriateness of the information they share, discerning between items suitable for the public arena and those that should stay more private. Of course, we don't assume that students will know how to make these kinds of decisions at the outset of the year; we teach them how to sort and we coach and check in throughout the year.

For example, we ask the class, "What can we do to be respectful when waiting for our turn to talk?" Or we reinforce appropriate sharing behavior: "Everyone spoke clearly and used audience voices today." We brainstorm questions that listeners can ask to elicit information and show curiosity about another's news or views. We generate a list of sentence starters that help listeners focus on the person sharing and demonstrate that they want to understand the sharer's perspective and care about what the sharer is saying. With our careful scaffolding, our guiding hand while they practice, and our feedback, students develop their abilities to compose and deliver their sharing and respond to others' sharing.

Perhaps the most difficult skill to learn in this arena is that of responding effectively to others' sharing. When a student says, "I bet you feel really happy that you can get your cast taken off tomorrow," or asks, "What's one special thing you're going to do on your trip to Florida?" what they are truly communicating is "I paid attention to you; I care about how you feel." Comments and questions like these require seeing things from another's perspective, otherwise known as perspective-taking. Perspective-taking is directly related to the first steps of the social information processing model—encoding and interpretation of social situations—as it helps one to interpret a social situation correctly and to respond in an appropriate way (O'Kearney et al. 2017). Whether the sharing is about something momentous or a more everyday occurrence, responding well requires stepping away from our own vantage point to imagine how another person feels and using constructive words and tones in response to what they said. Here's how that looked in one classroom:

> In Morning Meeting, Graham proudly shares that he had an "awesome" visit with his mother over the weekend. Graham's parents are divorced and he sees his mom only occasionally. The class listens intently while he describes his visit with her. His pleasure and excitement are evident in the details he reveals. He ends his sharing by stating, "I'm ready for questions and comments." Slowly, carefully, several hands go up. The first questions ask for more detail.
>
> "You said your mom gave you a present. What was it?"
>
> "What restaurant did you go to?"
>
> As the students get more comfortable, their questions and comments show their understanding—and their empathy.
>
> "Do you miss your mom a lot when she leaves?"
>
> "I think you really like seeing your mom."
>
> "What was the best part for you?"

"I met his mom," a classmate says. "She's nice." Graham's smile is wide and proud.

This is a simple but rich exchange, filled with expressions of interest and caring.

It doesn't always go so smoothly, of course. "We got a new puppy this weekend," shares kindergartner Tessa. "I'm ready for questions and comments." Hands shoot up around the circle. Tessa calls on Allie.

"I have a dog, too, and this morning he threw up on the rug," begins Allie, turning the attention away from the sharer and onto herself. She takes a breath as she prepares to launch into her tale.

Her teacher takes advantage of the pause. "Tomorrow when it's your turn to share, you can tell us about your dog. Right now, can you think of a question or a comment for Tessa about her news?"

Reminded, Allie certainly can. "I bet you like to play with him," she says. And sharing is back on track.

Sharing Teaches Thinking, Listening, and Speaking Skills

The research of many respected educational theorists, including Jean Piaget and Lev Vygotsky, has examined and documented the ways in which social interaction influences cognitive development (Rogoff 1990). Though Piaget and Vygotsky describe differing models of the relationship between the social and cognitive, both recognize the importance of developing the skills of stating one's thoughts with clarity, actively listening, and forming questions that elicit more information. These skills are crucial for students to learn if they're to be

Highlights of Sharing

- Provides an arena for students to share news and views

- Lets students learn about each other

- Offers practice in speaking to a partner and to a group

- Develops students' judgment of the appropriateness of sharing various kinds of news with different audiences

- Allows students to practice careful listening

- Offers students an engaging way to develop empathy, consideration of others' perspectives, and social awareness

- Helps students develop a repertoire of responses to different kinds of news, including asking constructive, purposeful questions and offering empathetic, insightful comments

- Enhances students' vocabulary development and reading success

successful with academics, meet the requirements of the Common Core State Standards, and flourish in our twenty-first century world. The beauty of sharing is that students practice these skills in meaningful ways that are integrated with the academic, social, and emotional content of their lives.

For many of us, our own school experiences with speaking to a group consisted only of formal, artificial situations and were seldom about anything of deep interest to us. Instead, we were assigned to do "oral reports" on designated topics, reports that were thinly disguised paraphrases of encyclopedia passages. We were encouraged to speak at length, and we often mumbled to disguise the fact that we couldn't pronounce many of the words we had painstakingly copied.

How wonderfully different sharing is! First of all, the material has intrinsic interest, and students can make choices even within structured topics. A teacher says, "We're going to do an around-the-circle sharing about a fun fact you learned in our study of rivers." Although the topic is named for them, each student gets to think about and name a personally appealing snippet of information from a recent lesson.

Sharing presentations are concise. Rather than learning to pad a presentation to stretch it out, students must synthesize information and then share enough to pique interest and give their audience a basis for response, while leaving room and reason for further inquiry and comment.

In small, low-stakes doses, sharing provides everyday practice in speaking to groups of different sizes. For example, students must speak in clear, audible voices when addressing the whole group, and they must modulate their volume when engaging in partner chats. When students can't hear a speaker, we teach a polite signal for "Turn up the volume," and students practice assertiveness when they use it.

Finally, to present their sharing to classmates, students must be able to choose words that convey information clearly and to craft and deliver a comprehensible narrative. When they don't, the feedback is immediate: "Wait a minute. I'm confused. When you say California is the biggest state, do you mean a lot of land or a lot of people?" Jared asks his classmate, Ruben, after Ruben has shared about the state he is studying. Ruben says, "I mean a lot of people," and then, after a pause, "So I guess I should say California is the most populous state." Ruben and the whole class have just gotten a mini-lesson on choosing precise words.

Being a productive member of the class during sharing requires that students listen to and remember what others say so that they can respond appropriately. Since the topics often spring from their direct experience, students are motivated to engage in the conversations, to hear each other.

Teachers also teach students that it's their job as listeners to formulate a question that elicits more information, or to make a comment that shows interest in the news presented or concern for the sharer—habits important for learning and for building relationships.

When Sadia asks Marcus, "How did you get the color in the flames to look so much like a real fire?" Marcus knows that Sadia has carefully observed his painting and that she really listened when he said that he was proud of the way he had blended colors in it.

Sharing Strengthens Language Development and Promotes Reading Success

Through Morning Meeting sharing, students build vocabulary, learn pronunciation, and learn to speak with grammatical accuracy. Equally as important, the conversations that take place during sharing help build students' background knowledge of a wide variety of topics, and that background knowledge helps them make sense of text when reading. In fact, researchers have recognized that all the conversational skills children learn and practice during Morning Meeting sharing—starting conversations, telling stories, listening, asking questions, commenting—are essential to literacy success (Goodson and Layzer 2009; Zwiers and Crawford 2011).

Some students may not recognize all of the words used during sharing conversations. In that case, teachers can define the words or help students use context clues to figure out words they don't know. Sometimes they spot and correct students' misunderstandings, as in the following third grade example:

> "On Saturday I went to Adventure World with my uncle. I went swimming there and I drowned," shares Regina.

> Her classmates are full of questions about her trip.

> "How long did it take to get there?"

> "Was there traffic?"

> "Was it scary when you drowned?"

> Wide-eyed and solemn, Regina nods emphatically. "It was really scary."

> Her teacher has listened and observed closely, and notices that many of the children share the same misunderstanding of this part of Regina's news.

> "Regina," she asks, "when you said that you drowned, did you mean that you had trouble swimming in the water?"

> Regina nods yes. An impromptu vocabulary lesson follows, a thread picked up from the fabric of Regina's sharing and woven seamlessly into the classroom circle.

> "*Drowned* is connected to having trouble in the water," affirms the teacher, "but it means that you had so much trouble that you died from not being able to get your face above the water to breathe."

The class listens intently. No embarrassment is attached to the mistake; they are glad to receive this information, given succinctly and matter-of-factly. It extends their ability to describe their own experiences and to interpret the experiences of others accurately in both oral communication and future texts they may encounter.

Getting Started

Here are some tips to help you as you implement the sharing component of Morning Meeting.

Browse the Sharing Ideas section on page 97 as you get started!

Introduce Simpler Types of Sharing First

It's the second day of school, and the fourth graders have just finished a simple greeting. The teacher waits until everyone is quiet and then says, "Today we're going to do sharing. I'm going to ask a question. We'll go around the circle and each of you will have a chance to answer the question. Who has done this kind of sharing in third grade?"

Several hands shoot up. "Okay. Today you will state one key idea in response to my question 'What is one thing you enjoy doing outside?' First, watch and notice what I do and say. 'Outside, I like to play catch with my son.' What did you notice about my sharing?"

Students respond, noticing that the teacher stuck to the key idea, spoke loudly, looked around the circle, and limited their sharing to only one sentence and one idea. These are all important skills, but for the purpose of this first sharing, what's most essential is having students keep their statements brief. This can be a difficult skill for loquacious fourth graders, so the "one idea" expectation is reinforced by saying, "Take a minute and think. What is one thing you enjoy doing outside? When you're ready, give a thumbs-up."

While children are thinking, a chart with a sentence stem ("Outside, I like to _____.") reminds them of the "one sentence" goal. As soon as all thumbs are up, the first day of sharing proceeds around the room.

Sharing is an essential part of Morning Meeting, introduced in the first days of school. In these early days, sharing is highly structured. Many teachers do around-the-circle sharing as a first experience. In around-the-circle sharing, as the example above shows, all members of the meeting circle share about a teacher-chosen topic. The around-the-circle structure provides a safe way to introduce basic sharing skills: how to decide on an idea to share, how to speak clearly, how to listen attentively and remember what was shared.

Other teachers might choose to do partner sharing first. In partner sharing, students pair up to talk with each other on a teacher-chosen topic. This is a good choice for a first sharing experience if many students are shy about speaking in front of the group or might get wiggly while others are speaking. Whether we begin with around-the-circle or partner sharing, teachers set the parameters carefully and provide ample support and guidance.

Introduce Dialogue Sharing as Skills Develop

As students' skills and comfort levels grow, we can introduce dialogue sharing, in which one person shares news or information with the entire class and then asks for questions and comments. To be successful with dialogue sharing, students need to share a main idea and supporting details, speak clearly, listen carefully, and offer thoughtful questions and comments.

Because dialogue sharing tends to be the hardest for students, it's usually the last format introduced, and the skills are taught gradually. Sometimes teachers use partner sharing as a bridge to dialogue sharing because partner sharing allows students to learn and practice many of the skills they'll need for dialogue sharing in a lower-risk format. Initially, the class does dialogue sharing on a teacher-chosen topic (also called a focused topic). Later, they can move to dialogue sharing with an open topic.

Throughout the Year, Choose the Best Format for the Day

Once the class is competent in all formats, teachers choose which format to use on a given day depending on students' needs, time constraints, and classroom events. For example, on a day when the teacher wants everyone to think and talk about a certain topic, they might use around-the-circle sharing. This can be a good format for Mondays when students are excited about weekend activities or caught up in current events that happened while they were apart.

On a subsequent day, partner sharing or dialogue sharing might provide a time for more in-depth conversations. For example, students could do a partner sharing or a focused-topic dialogue sharing about which book character they like best and why.

There's no prescription for how to pick and choose among these three formats as the year unfolds. Many teachers focus on dialogue sharing, recognizing that this format provides deep practice in speaking, listening, and thinking skills. Others might find that around-the-circle sharing or partner sharing most frequently suits students' needs. The bottom line is to do sharing in a way that offers an appropriate level of challenge and that allows all class members to feel heard and cared for in a safe environment.

Understand Sharing Responsibilities

In implementing and assessing sharing, keep the following general responsibilities in mind.

Teacher's responsibilities:

- Set up systems for dialogue sharing, such as signing up ahead of time on a schedule chart and designating the number of questions and comments allowed.
- Keep the process moving by acting as facilitator and timekeeper.
- Model good oral communication skills.
- Model appropriate language for questions and comments.
- Help students keep the focus on the sharer.
- Screen out or stop sharing that is inappropriate for the group.

Students' responsibilities:

- Choose news that is appropriate to share with the group.
- Organize their ideas and keep their sharing brief.
- Speak loudly and clearly.
- Look at the audience.
- Wait their turn to share.
- Put any objects they'll need for their sharing in the designated sharing place to avoid distracting themselves or others.
- Listen attentively when others are sharing.
- Offer questions and comments that are focused on the sharer and that show interest, respect, and caring.
- Respond appropriately to questions and comments.

Teach Essential Skills for Sharing

Sharing is complex, even in the highly structured around-the-circle and partner formats. In order to fulfill the responsibilities listed above, students need to think about what to say, formulate a complete and focused thought, and articulate it clearly. They also need to exert enough self-control to sit quietly while others talk, and they need to focus attention on the speaker. For these reasons, it's important to break sharing down into its component skills and to carefully teach each skill. All grade levels benefit from this explicit teaching—upper-grade teachers might assume that older students already know how to share and listen, but often they don't.

The jobs of the sharer include using a strong, clear voice, looking at the audience, and saying something brief, focused, and on topic. In the fourth grade around-the-circle sharing described above, the teacher began by teaching how to state one key idea. In subsequent days, she focused on speaking in a clear and audible voice; choosing appropriate, on-topic items to share; looking around at the entire audience, not just one person; using facial expression; and stating a main idea with supporting details.

Interactive Modeling (see page 27) is a key strategy to use in teaching all of these skills. Here are some additional strategies you might use to support students as they learn and practice sharing skills.

Brainstorm for Ideas

When you first introduce sharing on a focused topic, ask students to brainstorm possible responses. To give students some ideas to draw on, write their ideas on a chart before starting the sharing. For example, a first grade class brainstormed a list of favorite everyday places before doing an around-the-circle sharing. This served two purposes: it helped children stay on topic, and it enabled the teacher to guide children in naming truly everyday places, such as "my grandma's kitchen" or "our back porch." Consider drawing or putting up pictures of the ideas the class generates to support students who are still learning to read or speak English.

Use Sentence Stems

Posting a sentence stem that children complete will help them focus and also support them in learning to use complete sentences. This is especially useful in younger grades and with students who are English language learners. In a K–1 class, the sentence stem may be as simple as "A healthy food I like is _____." Sentence stems can also help older students stay on topic and formulate complex sentences. In a fifth grade class, the sentence stem might be "I connected with the character _____ from our book because _____."

Give Clear Directions

Setting clear parameters in your directions can help students stay focused. Instead of saying, "Tell about your animal habitat project," you can narrow things down by saying, "Share one thing you learned while doing your animal habitat project."

Use Think-Alouds

To model how to choose one idea among many, you might do a "think-aloud." Use a gesture such as putting a finger to your head to indicate that you're going to speak your thoughts, and then narrate a thought process through Interactive Modeling. Let's say the topic is "What I like to do on weekends." Your think-aloud might sound like this: "Hmm . . . I like to do lots of different things. I like to go to the farmers market, sometimes I go to the movies, and it's fun to go walking in the park because I can take my dog. I know some of the other kids have dogs—maybe that's what I'll share."

Teach Essential Skills for Listening

In all forms of sharing, listeners need to stay quiet, maintain self-control, and demonstrate attentive listening. As the class's sophistication with sharing evolves, listeners need to remember what was said, formulate questions that show interest and elicit more information, and make empathetic comments. Here is a possible sequence of listening skills to teach. Introduce each skill as students show readiness to take their sharing to the next level of complexity.

Remembering Details

Before students begin an around-the-circle sharing, tell them to listen carefully to what their classmates say because they'll be playing "Who Remembers?" afterward. Give them a minute to think of a strategy they can use to remember what is said. Then, when everyone has shared, ask questions to prompt recall. For example, if the sharing was about a favorite book, ask questions such as "Who remembers whose favorite book was *Twister on Tuesday*?" or "Who remembers who named a nonfiction book as their favorite?" When the class has done this activity a few times, you could ask students to come up with the questions.

As a next step, have listeners remember details of what was shared during partner sharing or focused-topic dialogue sharing. For example, after fourth grader Serena finished a dialogue sharing about teaching her dog new tricks, the teacher said, "Raise your hand if you can name one thing you heard Serena say." Students responded, "Her dog's name is Marley." "Her dog is twelve years old." "She taught her dog two new tricks." "One of the tricks she taught her dog was how to shake." Students continued to respond until they had named all the things they'd heard Serena say.

A variation on remembering details is to ask listeners to summarize what the sharer said. You can introduce this variation during partner sharing using an assigned topic. Everyone shares about the topic with their partner. Then, going around the circle, students take turns summarizing for the whole group what their partner said.

Generating Effective Questions

Effective questions reflect the spirit of sharing in that they acknowledge and encourage the sharer. You can introduce the skill of asking questions during a partner sharing (when students will be asking questions to learn about each other) or during a dialogue sharing. Begin by discussing what makes an effective question. Be sure the following points are covered:

- Effective questions show interest in the sharer and their news.

- They can be about either the factual or the emotional content of the sharing.

- They often elicit new information and extend understanding.

- They sometimes clarify information.

- They are positive and supportive rather than challenging.

Post a list of question words (see sample chart at right) and give students an opportunity to practice using them. You could share a quick story or an opinion about a topic the class is interested in and then have them use the question words to generate questions about what they heard.

Remind and encourage students to use the question words during partner sharing or dialogue sharing. When you first introduce question asking during dialogue sharing with younger students, help them along by having the class pause before the sharer invites questions. As a class, brainstorm possible questions using the question words you've posted. Then return to the sharing format and let the sharer signal when they are ready for questions. With older students, you could simply refer to a posted list of question starters to remind them of the kinds of questions to ask.

With older students, a sticky note strategy can also be helpful: after a student shares, pass out a sticky note and pencil to each student. Working with a partner, they each write down an interesting question to ask (being sure to sign the note) and give the note to the sharer. The sharer then chooses three or four questions to answer aloud; remaining questions are posted on a sharing chart by the circle area to be answered individually when the sharer has time.

Question Words

Who Who helped you with that?
Who was with you when this happened?

_____

What What was your favorite part about _____?
What made you excited [happy, sad] about that?

_____

When When do you think you will _____?
When would you like to _____?

_____

Where Where did this take place?
Where do you want to go next time?

_____

Why Why do you think _____?
Why did you decide to _____?

_____

How How did you feel about that?
How did they respond when you _____?

Making Empathetic Comments

Making empathetic comments offers unique opportunities for students to practice important academic and social skills. Students need to listen attentively; observe and interpret a classmate's words, body language, and tone; remember what was said; and formulate a relevant and respectful observation or affirmation.

Of all the skills involved in sharing, offering empathetic comments is perhaps the hardest to learn. It requires taking another's perspective and thinking about what will help that person feel heard and cared for. Because this ability develops as children mature, younger children tend to have more difficulty offering comments than older children.

Here's a suggested sequence for introducing commenting:

1. **Discuss what a comment is and what makes a good comment.** Make sure the following points are made:

- Takes the form of a statement rather than a question

- Helps the sharer feel listened to and supported

- Focuses on the sharer rather than on the responder; this point is especially important for younger students, who are usually eager to share their own experiences in response to a classmate's sharing ("I have a puppy, too!")

- Might notice and appreciate a detail from the sharing

- Might respond to how the sharer feels; listeners will need to pay attention to body language, facial expression, and tone along with words so that they can make comments of this type

2. **Brainstorm empathetic comments.** Briefly share something with the class, being sure to convey emotion along with interesting details. For example: "Late yesterday afternoon when I was starting to make dinner for my family, I heard a loud bang and heard my daughter scream. I ran toward the front door, and she told me that our dog, Shennah, had figured out how to open the front door and was loose in the neighborhood. There's a busy street nearby, and I was worried that Shennah might be heading that way. I ran all over the neighborhood and was so relieved when I finally found her at the park chasing some squirrels." After telling your story, ask students to brainstorm a list of comments that either note details about what you said or note how you felt, being sure to keep the focus on you and your news. As students brainstorm, write their sentence starters on a chart: "It seems like you felt . . ." "I bet you were wondering . . ." "It sounds like you . . ." Then ask students what these comments have in common. They'll probably soon discover that all the comments include the word *you*—in other words, the focus stays on the sharer. Keep this chart posted by the meeting circle for students to use as a reference.

3. **Separate questions from comments at the next Morning Meeting.** At the next meeting, do a dialogue sharing and bring in commenting, but keep it separate from question asking. Have the class brainstorm a list of comments in response to each sharing. Then, after all comments have been voiced, sharers can say, "I am ready for questions."

4. **Model and practice how to respond respectfully to a comment.** Just as it's important for listeners to offer empathetic comments, it's important that sharers respond respectfully to those comments. Model how to do this. For example, for the loose dog story, you might go back to the class's brainstormed comments and give some respectful responses: "Yes, I was feeling really worried about my dog; I thought a car might have hit her," "I do feel lucky that nothing happened to her," or just a simple "Thank you" and a nod. After your modeling, give students a chance to practice respectfully acknowledging a comment.

5. **Put it all together.** The final step is to have the audience give both comments and questions during partner and dialogue sharing. Listeners now need to incorporate all the questioning and commenting skills they've practiced, and sharers must deploy all they've learned about answering questions and responding to comments.

Sharing Skills to Teach, Model, and Practice

Introduce during around-the-circle sharing	Speak in a clear voice. Look at the audience when speaking. State one main idea. Stay on topic. Listen quietly and respectfully while others are speaking. Remember details of what was shared.
Introduce during partner sharing	State one main idea with supporting details. Ask friendly questions to elicit more information. Make empathetic comments.
Introduce during dialogue sharing	Sign up to share. Choose appropriate topics for open-topic sharing. Initiate questions and comments. As an audience member, raise hand to speak, and speak only when called on.

To learn more about teaching these skills in elementary school, see *The Language of Learning: Teaching Students Core Thinking, Listening, and Speaking Skills* by Margaret Berry Wilson (Center for Responsive Schools, 2015).

Scan the QR code to see a teacher show her students how to offer comments.

Pay Attention to the Focus and Flow of Sharing

An important teacher role during sharing is to help students stay focused and maintain a comfortable conversational give-and-take. In around-the-circle sharing, teachers often need to help the class stay on topic. You can proactively address this by being clear about the topic and by modeling—and re-modeling—how to share one key idea. When individuals do stray off topic or start to share a whole story, remind them of the topic and the one-idea limit.

In dialogue sharing, common challenges are making sure that all sharers get responses and that all students, rather than the same few, offer questions and comments. If you notice problems in these areas, it's important to address them directly and give students a chance to think about and practice the skills involved.

For example, you might begin by naming the problem: "Although sharing has been interesting, sharers haven't been getting many questions and comments." You could then lead a brief discussion to build empathy for how actions, intentional or not, can make someone feel. "How does it feel when you're sharing and only a couple of people raise their hands with questions or comments?" After taking a few responses, name your expectation for all: "I know it can be hard sometimes to come up with questions and comments in the moment, but that is the job of the audience."

Remind sharers that they need to use a phrase such as "I am ready for questions and comments" rather than asking if there are any questions. This signals the expectation that there will be questions and comments. Then, give a refresher lesson: just as when you first taught the class about questioning and commenting, share something interesting with the class and have them brainstorm and practice offering both questions and comments.

It is important to end on an encouraging note, reinforcing students' efforts during the lesson and reiterating the expectations for future sharing: "Wow. We brainstormed eleven questions and seven comments. The rest of this week, I'll be watching for all of you to be thinking hard about what else would be interesting to find out from sharers and what thoughtful responses you can offer them."

Direct the Content of Sharing as Needed to Keep It Inclusive

It's important to take an active role in directing the content of sharing, even—or especially—when it is open-topic sharing. Obviously, we don't want to stifle children from sharing about special events in their lives, but we do want to avoid having them share things that highlight advantages and shut out less advantaged classmates.

One way we can address this is by helping students identify and share about topics that don't involve objects or special opportunities based on economics. For example, after winter break, you might have students share about "a favorite memory" or "a special time you spent with someone" rather than "a favorite gift."

One teacher even used Morning Meeting sharing time to have students discuss the issue of economics and the holidays head-on. In an around-the-circle sharing in early December, she asked the class, "Do you have to give something expensive for a gift to be valuable? What's one idea of a gift you could give that doesn't cost anything?" Later she reflected: "I was so moved by their responses. A lot of these kids' families don't have much money. They came up with wonderful ideas! Things that they could make, things that they already had and would like to share. They suggested the gift of time—of being there to really listen to someone."

In classes of younger children, "bring and brag" syndrome is often a problem throughout the year. Many teachers avoid this by establishing a general "no toys for sharing" rule. Recognizing, however, that sometimes it's important to have a chance to share a special item, other teachers occasionally do "category sharing"—choosing a category of things that they're sure most children will have, such as "Bring Your Favorite Stuffie Week" or "Bring Something You Liked to Play With as a Baby Week."

Teach Students What News Is Appropriate to Share With the Class

For the purposes of Morning Meeting, teach students to sort the news in their lives into two overall categories—community news and private family news.

Community news is appropriate for the classroom community to hear; private family news is not appropriate for sharing with the whole class. The latter category could include information that is confidential from a legal or ethical viewpoint or details a child has overheard about a court case a family member is involved in, or it might include a complicated family situation, such as a divorce or family dispute.

Let students know that they can share private family news with you, their teacher, but not the whole class. Making this distinction not only protects the student and their family but also protects the rest of the class from access to information that is beyond their capacity to cope with or understand.

Affirm that sometimes it's hard to decide whether certain news is suitable for group sharing, and make sure students know that if in doubt, they can always check with you. One teacher tells her class, "If something is really troubling you, it might upset other students as well. Talk to me before you share information like this with the class."

Also helpful is brainstorming a list of appropriate news items and posting the list near the meeting circle. You can then refer students to this list as they prepare to do open-topic dialogue sharing. You might begin such a brainstorming session by asking, "If sharing is a time to get to know each other better, what types of information might you share?" Students list things such as hobbies, family, pets, books they like, something especially interesting they learned recently at school, something they learned at school that they have questions about, a special memory, friends, and so on. You can continue adding ideas to this chart throughout the year.

Finally, if a student begins to share news that you realize is inappropriate, intervene. For example, Katy's mother is a reporter for the town newspaper. One day, Katy began to share details of a recent crime that she'd heard her mother talk about. Knowing that this was straying into dicey territory, the teacher stopped her. "Katy, I'd like you to hold on to the rest of your sharing until I can talk with you about it later. I'm not sure that it's news for our whole class to hear." She then made sure to talk with Katy soon after the meeting.

Prepare Students to Handle the Sharing of Serious News

Within the "community news" category are many light, humorous, and matter-of-fact topics. But community news may also sometimes be sad and painful or worrisome. When the classroom climate is safe and comfortable, both kinds of news can be offered and received with care and respect.

Younger children tend to blurt out what they need to say when they need to say it. With the help of their teacher, however, they are able to recognize that some news is serious and demands a different kind of response than other, lighter news. As teachers, we can model a response: "I'm sorry to hear that your dad is in the hospital."

Older children can be more deliberate about the sharing of serious news. Some teachers of older children introduce labels for the two types of community news—general news and serious news, for example. When a class first begins doing Morning Meeting sharing, most news offered tends to be general news: new pets, visits to or from family members, sports games or other events in which students have participated, and so forth. When class members are at ease with the structures of sharing, questions, and comments, and when they trust each other to respond easily and respectfully to general news, you might inform the group that they are ready to add serious news: illnesses or deaths in the family, upsetting events in the community, natural disasters, and so on.

Emphasize to students that they should always bring serious news to you first and you will determine whether it's appropriate to share with the group. In some cases, you may need to help a student modify the serious news to make it appropriate; in other cases, you may need to explain to a student that the news is not suitable to share with the class. Let parents know ahead of time that you will be introducing serious news and that you will be carefully filtering any serious news students bring in.

Through discussion and brainstorming, help the class sort and categorize their news. What are some examples of general news? Serious news? It's also helpful to generate ideas for constructive responses to different kinds of news: "If someone shares something sad," you might ask, "what can we say to let them know that we listened well and that we care how they feel?"

These are not skills commonly taught. Even as well-intentioned adults, we often struggle to find the "right" words. Too often, our awkwardness and discomfort can cause us to avoid acknowledging another's pain or offering our help. The practice provided by responding to news during sharing can help students feel more competent at navigating these situations.

Make Sure Questions and Comments Are Caring and Empathetic

An incident in a first grade classroom highlights the importance of the teacher's role in directing the tone of questions and comments, be they in response to serious, lighthearted, excited, or matter-of-fact sharings:

It was December, only a few days before the holiday vacation, and the six-year-olds in Ms. Donnelly's classroom were spilling over with the excitement of the season.

When the time came for dialogue sharing, Anthony was the first to share. His words flew out fast and excited. "My grandma's coming from Italy to visit me!"

"He already told us that!" blurted Adam. It was a thoroughly six-year-old retort, impulsive and tinged with righteous indignation at having to hear something twice. It was not meant to be unkind, though it fell with a cruel thud upon the enthusiastic Anthony.

Instead of directly chastising Adam, Ms. Donnelly asked a question. "Why might Anthony want to tell us again that his grandma is coming? What would make a person repeat news?"

Several ideas were ventured. "I say things twice when I'm really excited!"

"Maybe Anthony's got more to tell than when he told it the first time."

"Probably 'cause it's really important news to him."

Ms. Donnelly nodded and then handed the reins back to Anthony. "Okay, Anthony, you can choose people for questions and comments." Questions abounded:

"How long since you saw her?"

"When's she coming?"

"Is she gonna bring you a present from Italy?"

Ms. Donnelly made the final comment. "Maybe, Anthony, your grandma could come to school with you."

Without the guidance of their teacher, this group of six-year-olds would probably have been unable to move beyond their concern about the detail of Adam's observation into a contemplation based upon empathy for Anthony. More likely, their diversion into "who said what when" would have prevented them from responding to Anthony's news at all.

The teacher's intervention and response to Adam's comment let the whole class know that the important thing was to think about Anthony and respond to his news in a caring way. But she did this in a way that did not highlight Adam or his blunder. He stood corrected, but gently and quickly, giving him space to learn from his mistake. Moreover, because Ms. Donnelly invited everyone to help solve the puzzle of why a person might share the same news twice, the discovery was not limited to the two children directly involved but instead became a spontaneous whole-class lesson in empathy and understanding people's motivations.

Common Questions

Q **What should I do when a student doesn't speak loudly enough for others to hear or when the class can't understand a particular child? Should I repeat that child's words?**

A Though these situations call for individual judgment, a general guideline is to resist "voice-overs." Allow sharers to speak for themselves unless a severe speech problem or some other issue clearly creates communication difficulties. Make sure students know and use courteous ways of telling a classmate that they didn't hear or understand something that was said.

One educator struggled with this issue when teaching second graders, who tend to be quiet and unassertive. She wanted to empower children to take charge of their own learning and to communicate when they couldn't hear or understand what someone was saying. The class created a "Turn it up" signal that anyone could use (extend your arm, make a fist with thumb to the side, and then turn your fist so the thumb points up). And when children heard but didn't understand another child's words, they would say, "Could you repeat that, please? I didn't catch all your words."

Q **Is it all right for me to ask questions and make comments, or should I leave that to the students?**

A It is definitely all right for you to ask questions and offer comments. In fact, it's vital for students to see that you find their news interesting and that you care about how things are going for them. It's also a good opportunity to model questions and comments in an unobtrusive way.

However, it's best to allow students to respond first. Also, avoid responding to every single sharing. If you do, the message is that an exchange isn't really valid unless the teacher has spoken.

Q **I know I should discourage responses that shift the focus onto the responder— comments like "I have a cat too, and . . . " But sometimes these seem like honest attempts at connection and empathy, not simple self-centeredness. Is it ever okay to allow such comments?**

A This question involves a judgment call we must make as we guide sharing. Is the intention of the response to highlight a connection with the sharer and acknowledge a bond revealed by the sharing? Or is the intention to divert the focus from the sharer to the responder and their news?

Like many distinctions, this is not always clear and tidy. What begins as an acknowledgment of connection can slide quickly into one's own sharing. When that happens, the teacher needs to stop the commenting child with a respectful reminder: "That sounds like some interesting information about you, Chris. You could share it tomorrow when it's your turn. Now you can ask Bruce a question or make a comment about his sharing."

Signaling Shared Connections

One way to show a connection to what a speaker is saying without interrupting them or shifting the focus to yourself is to use the "Me, too!" hand signal. To use this signal, fold down your middle three fingers, extending your thumb and pinkie, and move your hand back and forth toward the sharer and yourself, pointing your thumb toward yourself and your pinkie toward the other person.

The goal is to help students respond to another's experience without bringing the attention back to themselves. We want to keep the spotlight on the sharer. Some teachers model and practice with students a specific "Me, too!" signal they can use to indicate a shared connection with the speaker. Along with teaching a signal, you can also discuss times students could talk more about shared interests and experiences. For example, ask students, "When might be a good time to talk about our connections? What could you say if you wanted to talk to someone later in the day about your shared interest?"

Q **When children bring in an object to share, they often can't find it when it's their turn to share. Or everyone in the circle wants to touch the object. Sometimes arguments occur over how the object is handled. How can I keep the child's sharing from getting lost in the shuffle?**

A Sharing objects can create lots of problems in addition to the "bring and brag" syndrome previously discussed. If you're going to have children bring in objects for sharing, you can use various strategies to keep the objects from becoming distractions. One is to designate a "show shelf" or "sharing basket" in the room. When children bring in an object for sharing, they leave it in this spot where others are able to view it but not touch it.

Once the object is shared, it's put back on the shelf until the end of the day. If the sharer wants children to handle the object later in the day, the sharer can explain and demonstrate during sharing how the object should be handled. Finally, as a general rule, don't allow objects to be passed around the circle. It usually takes a very long time, during which the focus is shifted from the sharer to the object itself.

Q Sharing can be daunting to students with limited English proficiency or verbal skills. How can I support them while keeping sharing meaningful?

A Around-the-circle sharing provides a lot of support and allows students with limited verbal or English proficiency skills to hear many similar statements on the same topic. You can further support students by giving them the opportunity to preview their topic with you or a paraprofessional. As an additional scaffold, you can substitute around-the-circle sharing with partner sharing. In partner sharing, students need to speak in front of only one person, which reduces risk. Even dialogue sharing can be manageable with some simple supports. Here are a few ideas:

- **Have students rehearse beforehand.** Sharing doesn't need to be spontaneous speech. You, a paraprofessional, or other students in the class can work with students outside of Morning Meeting to help them prepare for sharing.

- **Avoid topics that might elicit negative responses.** Sharing promotes connection, but certain topics can elicit strong emotions for some students. Rely on your knowledge of your students as you plan sharing topics.

- **Use sentence starters or fill-in-the-blank cues.** Let's say you're doing a focused-topic sharing in which students choose three things to tell about themselves, such as, "I like math. I have a guinea pig. I play basketball." To make this easier, you can give students a fill-in-the-blank sentence format: "I like to eat _____. I come from _____. My favorite color is _____."

- **Use props.** Plan sharings in which students bring in a photo or other item from home, hold it up, and then respond to questions. At first, you can restrict the questions to ones that invite simple yes-or-no answers. As students begin to learn vocabulary, the supportive environment of sharing will give them wonderful opportunities to practice speaking and gain fluency.

- **Share classwork.** Sharing class projects or artwork is a simple way for all students to participate in sharing. Before Morning Meeting, they can work with you or a classmate to prepare and practice brief descriptive statements about the project or artwork.

Sharing Ideas

The sharing ideas on the following pages are flexible: they can be adapted for a range of ages and purposes and for different times of the year. Feel free to use them as is or modify them to meet students' needs.

Most of the ideas can be used at multiple grade levels with modifications in the level of challenge. For example, in the around-the-circle sharing Favorites (page 101), younger students might be most successful responding with a word or simple phrase, whereas older students could use complete sentences and perhaps add information about why something is a favorite.

Ideas that work well for older students early in the year might not be appropriate for younger students until midyear or later, when they've had time to learn basic sharing skills and any relevant content knowledge. For example, if you teach older students, you might have them mix and mingle (page 98) to pair them up right from the beginning of the year. But if you teach younger students, you might want to wait until later in the year when they've had more opportunities to practice self-control and responding to signals for quiet.

With some modification, the same sharing idea can be used to meet a range of academic and social purposes. For example, you can use the What We Have in Common partner chat (page 107) to have students name common questions they have about some recently learned content or name common interests they have outside of school.

Partner Sharing

Partner sharing can be done with the ideas in this section and with many other topics. Mix and match the structures with topics. In time, you'll see which combinations best engage and stretch your class. Here are some ways to put students together for partner sharing, starting with simpler structures and building up to more challenging ones:

- **Assign Partners**—Purposefully assign each student a partner for sharing. To create pairs, consider the social and academic skills students need to practice or stretch. For example, does the class need to build greater cohesiveness? Perhaps pairing students with classmates they don't usually interact with will help. Is the class in the middle of a research project? Pairing students who are researching similar topics can spark ideas and enthusiasm.

- **Pair Up With a Neighbor**—Students simply pair up with the person to their right or left in the circle. Partners take turns talking about the chosen topic. After a few minutes, if time and students' skills permit, you might invite a few students to tell the whole class something their partner said.

- **Inside-Outside Circles**—Have students count off by twos. The ones form an inner circle and face out. The twos form an outer circle and face in, so pairs of students are now facing each other. Give students a topic to discuss, such as what they like studying in school and why. Allow students one minute to share with their partners. On your signal, the outside circle moves one person to the right while the inside circle stays in place, and everyone shares with a new partner. Repeat as many rounds as time allows. As students become comfortable with this structure, you can change topics each time they change partners. You can also vary which circle moves and in which direction.

- **Mix and Mingle**—To begin, students mix and mingle in the center of the circle. When you ring a chime, they pause and pair up with a student near them. Once everyone has a partner, give them a topic to discuss (for example, favorite holiday tradition, how they are similar to or different from the main character in a book they're reading, what they found most interesting in yesterday's discussion of World War II). After a minute or two, ring the chime again, and students once again mix and mingle until you signal that it's time to find a new partner. Continue through several rounds. Challenge students to pair up with people who are not their usual partners or best friends. Topics can be either social or academic.

- **Maître d'**—Tell students that you will pretend to be the maître d' in a restaurant and will call out groupings, such as "Table for two" or "Table for three." When you name a grouping, students form the specified groups. Once everyone is in a group, give them a topic to discuss (for example, favorite costume, prediction about what will happen in a read-aloud book, something they're looking forward to, ways they use math in everyday life). After a short time, ring a chime and call out a new grouping. Students regroup and you name a new topic to discuss. Challenge students to form groups with classmates they don't usually talk with.

Dialogue Sharing

When introducing dialogue sharing, consider using the following structures to set students up for success. Both can be used with a specific topic you assign or with an open-topic format that lets students choose what to share about.

Scan the QR code to see a dialogue sharing in action.

- **Sharing Jar**—This structure helps students learn to state a main idea and supporting details. Place in front of you an empty container, a lid for the container, and five items such as math counters, cubes, or marbles in three different colors (for example, one green item for the main idea, three yellow items for supporting details, one red item for a concluding statement). Introduce and model the sharing. For example:

    ○ On the weekends, I enjoy scrapbooking. (Put the green item in the container.)

○ I love to look through my photos and decide how to put them in my scrapbook. (Put a yellow item in the container.)

○ Then I find some stickers to go with my photos. (Put another yellow item in the container.)

○ Finally, I write a fun caption for each photo. (Put a third yellow item in the container.)

○ I feel proud when I've finished a scrapbook page. (Put the red item in the container and place the lid on the jar.)

Continue to use the sharing jar until students become more comfortable with the main-idea-and-supporting-details structure.

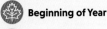

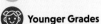

- **Who Can Name One Thing I Said?**—This structure helps students focus on the specifics in a classmate's sharing. Let students know that as the sharer speaks, their job as listeners is to pay attention and remember key details. Sharers state a main idea and several supporting details and then ask, "Who can remember one thing I said?" They then call on students one at a time to state just one detail until all key details have been recalled. Variation for younger children: Sharers hold up a photo or drawing (of a family pet, for example) and say three things about it. They then ask, "Who can name one thing I said?" and call on up to three people to respond.

Sharing	PAGE	Beginning of Year	Later in Year	Younger Grades	Older Grades	Around-the-Circle Sharing	Partner Sharing	Dialogue Sharing	Academic Content Reinforcement
Character Connection	100	✓	✓	✓	✓	✓	✓	✓	✓
Chocolate Chips for All!	100	✓		✓	✓	✓	✓		
Class Rocks	101	✓		✓		✓			
Favorites	101	✓		✓	✓	✓			
Headlines!	102		✓		✓	✓			
If I Were One Inch Tall	102	✓		✓	✓	✓			✓
It Could Be a . . .	103		✓	✓	✓	✓			✓
My Partner's Future	103		✓	✓	✓		✓		
Something I Learned . . .	104		✓	✓	✓	✓			✓
Take a Walk	104		✓	✓			✓		
This or That	105			✓			✓		
Tomorrow's Technology	106		✓		✓			✓	✓
What Can We Share About?	106	✓		✓	✓	✓			
What We Have in Common	107		✓		✓		✓		
Years of Trash	107		✓		✓	✓			✓

Sharing for:

 Beginning of Year

 Later in Year

 Younger Grades

 Older Grades

 Around-the-Circle Sharing

 Partner Sharing

 Dialogue Sharing

Academic Content Reinforcement

Character Connection

1. This activity can be done using around-the-circle sharing, partner sharing, or dialogue sharing. Have students sit in a circle or pair up, or decide who will share today, depending on the format you use.

2. Each person names the book they're reading, names a character who interests them, and says how the character connects to their life. Model the sharing: "I read *Freak the Mighty* by Rodman Philbrick. I connected with Max because his friends are very important to him, just like mine are to me. He walked over ten miles to the hospital to see his sick friend when no one would drive him there."

3. If doing as a partner sharing, call on a few student volunteers to share with the entire class what their partner said. If doing as a dialogue sharing, have sharers take questions and comments.

Chocolate Chips for All!

1. What are some ways you like to eat chocolate chips?

2. On chart paper or an interactive whiteboard, post photos of a few different ways people eat chocolate chips. (Examples include cookies, pancakes, ice cream, etc.)

3. With a partner, students share how they like to eat chocolate chips. Their response could be one of the options provided, or another way. Give students two or three minutes to chat, and then allow a few to share with the whole group if there is time.

Variations:

- This sharing could be done as an around-the-circle share where each person shares what their favorite is in one sentence: "I like to eat chocolate chips in ____."

- This sharing could be done with any food item!

Class Rocks

1. Before the day of the sharing, ask students to bring in a small rock that they find outside or near their home.

2. Give students practice in observation by challenging them to notice their rock's characteristics (for example, texture, color, grain size).

3. Going around the circle, each student presents their rock, tells where they found it, and names one characteristic about it. Model the sharing: "I found this rock in a park near my home. It has a smooth texture."

4. After everyone has shared, ask reflective questions that help students practice comparison and categorization skills: "What did you notice about our rocks?" "What do our rocks have in common?" "How might we sort these rocks into groups?"

Favorites

1. Name a category, such as vegetables, colors, numbers, foods, games, books, or songs. (You can write a question on the morning message chart to preview the category: "Be ready to share a favorite _____ during Morning Meeting.")

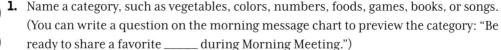

2. Going around the circle, each student names a favorite item in the chosen category. Depending on age and skill level, students can use just one word, a short phrase, or a complete sentence. Model how to do the sharing. When students are first using complete sentences, you can post a sentence stem for added support: "My favorite vegetable is _____."

3. After a student shares, invite the rest of the class to make the "Me, too!" sign if they like the same thing.

4. To extend this sharing, tally the favorites and use the data for a graphing activity later.

Sharing for:

 Beginning of Year

 Later in Year

 Younger Grades

 Older Grades

 Around-the-Circle Sharing

 Partner Sharing

 Dialogue Sharing

 Academic Content Reinforcement

Headlines!

1. In advance, give students index cards and invite them to write a headline about themselves (for example, "This Weekend Brings a Surprise Visitor," "*Bud, Not Buddy* Is a Favorite Book," "Family Reunion Planned for Next Summer"). Students should not put their names on their cards.

2. Collect and shuffle the cards and pass out one to each student.

3. Going around the circle, each student reads aloud the headline on their card and guesses who wrote it. If a student doesn't guess correctly after a couple of tries, the headline writer stands and says, "That's me!"

4. After everyone has read a card, prompt students to learn more about their classmates during other times of the school day, such as lunch and recess.

If I Were One Inch Tall

1. A fun prelude to this sharing is to read Shel Silverstein's poem "One Inch Tall" with the class.

2. Going around the circle, each student completes the sentence "If I were one inch tall, I would _____." Challenge students to be inventive and thoughtful in their responses. Model an example, such as "If I were one inch tall, I would use a toothpick as a vaulting pole."

Variation: Before students start to share, let them know that you'll play a quick game of "Who Remembers?" right after everyone has shared. Ask questions such as "Who remembers someone who shared what they would eat?" "Who remembers someone who shared what they would do outside?"

Variation: Use other measurements ("If I were one centimeter tall . . ." "If I were one meter tall . . .").

It Could Be a . . .

1. In the middle of the circle, display several shapes that students have been learning about in math. Write a sentence frame on a chart or the board: "I know this is a _____ [shape], but it could be a _____ [item that has that shape]."

2. Choose one shape and model the sharing. For example: "I know this is a cylinder, but it could be my new pencil holder."

3. Go around the circle with each student choosing a shape and doing a similar sharing.

Variation: Before you begin, let students know that you'll be asking them to remember what their classmates shared. Right after the last student has shared, ask questions to see how many different ideas the class can remember for each shape and list those on a chart. Encourage students to add new ideas to the chart throughout the day.

My Partner's Future

1. Pair up students and tell them that they will each name a career they're interested in and why. (For younger students, this can be phrased as what they want to be when they grow up.) For example: "I want to be a veterinarian because I love all kinds of animals" or "I want to be an author because I love to read and write stories."

2. After students talk together, each student summarizes for the whole class what their partner said.

Something I Learned . . .

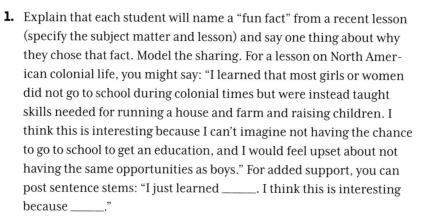

Sharing for:

 Beginning of Year

 Later in Year

 Younger Grades

 Older Grades

 Around-the-Circle Sharing

 Partner Sharing

 Dialogue Sharing

Academic Content Reinforcement

1. Explain that each student will name a "fun fact" from a recent lesson (specify the subject matter and lesson) and say one thing about why they chose that fact. Model the sharing. For a lesson on North American colonial life, you might say: "I learned that most girls or women did not go to school during colonial times but were instead taught skills needed for running a house and farm and raising children. I think this is interesting because I can't imagine not having the chance to go to school to get an education, and I would feel upset about not having the same opportunities as boys." For added support, you can post sentence stems: "I just learned _____. I think this is interesting because _____."

2. Give students some think time. When they're ready to share, have them give a thumbs-up.

3. Take the first turn yourself, then go around the circle having each student share their fun fact and reasoning for why they chose it.

4. After each student shares, the rest of the class has an opportunity to make a connection using the "Me, too!" sign.

 Take a Walk

1. A day or two before doing this focused-topic sharing, take students on a walk to find an object to bring back to class (or ask them to bring in an object from home). Tell them the rules for these objects: they must be safe, okay to take, and small enough to fit in their hand. You may also want to have a few objects handy, such as various leaves and rocks, in case students forget theirs.

2. Model how to succinctly share a main idea and a couple of supporting details about the object: "I chose this stick because it still has an acorn on it. That makes me think of the oak tree in my backyard. I love all the leaves that come off that tree in the fall. We rake a huge pile of leaves and jump in them for hours."

3. Call on the day's sharers. Spread this sharing out over several days so that all students get a chance to talk about the object they found.

This or That

1. Label chart paper with two headings: This and That.

2. Post photos of two related ideas under the labels.

3. Have students name whether they would prefer this or that. For example, post a picture of an apple and a banana. Ask students if they would prefer this (apple) or that (banana). In a partner sharing, students share their choice and why they made that choice.

Variation: Once students have shared, take raised hand votes for each choice and tally the total. Later, students can create a pie chart or bar graph to represent the answers.

Sharing for:

 Beginning of Year

 Later in Year

 Younger Grades

 Older Grades

 Around-the-Circle Sharing

 Partner Sharing

 Dialogue Sharing

 Academic Content Reinforcement

Tomorrow's Technology

1. In advance (perhaps during the previous day's science class), challenge students to think about items they use and ways to make them better (for example, a lunch box that keeps food cold far longer than the typical lunch box). To emphasize the science connection, introduce the sharing by saying, "Scientists and engineers think about how to improve things so that they use less energy, cost less to make, and so on. Beginning today, each of you will have a chance to share an idea for making something you use even better."

2. Model for students: "Something I use a lot is hand lotion. I would like to design a device that goes in the lotion bottle and makes sure you can get all the lotion out. I always feel like I waste so much because I can't get all of it out."

3. Call on the day's sharers. Spread this sharing out over several days so that all students get a chance to talk about their ideas.

4. As students share, you could record their ideas for use in another lesson.

What Can We Share About?

1. Let the class know that they'll be identifying topics that they can share about throughout the year. Provide examples of appropriate topics—such as, favorite foods, favorite games, pets, a piece of schoolwork, and so on.

2. Go around the circle with each student suggesting one topic. Write ideas on a chart, redirecting as needed if anyone names an inappropriate topic.

3. Post this list in the meeting circle and add to it as new topics arise.

What We Have in Common

1. Pair students with someone they don't usually work or play with.

2. Partners chat for about two minutes with the goal of discovering two things they have in common. Challenge them to go beyond the obvious. For example, instead of saying that they're both wearing jeans, students might learn through chatting that they both participate in gymnastics after school. To help students meet this challenge, you could brainstorm with them beforehand to generate a list of questions that will help them discover commonalities.

3. At a signal, students stop their conversation and together plan and practice how they'll share one of their commonalities with the whole class. When all are ready, go around the circle and have each pair name one commonality.

Variation: When doing this variation, plan for a shorter greeting and group activity (or use this as a combined sharing and group activity). In advance, make copies of blank Venn diagrams for students to fill out with partners. Pairs then find out not only what they have in common but also a few things that are unique to each of them. With a student volunteer, model the conversation (for example, discuss books, music, family members, and favorites) and also demonstrate how to fill out the Venn diagram as you talk. If time permits, ask each pair to share with the class one thing they have in common. You may also want to collect the completed Venn diagrams for later use.

Scan the QR code to download a printable Venn diagram template.

Years of Trash

1. Ahead of time, tell students to bring an item of trash from their home or neighborhood. The item should be safe and sanitary, likely to last for one hundred years in a landfill, and represent something about themselves or their family or community. Brainstorm suitable examples, such as product packaging, used gift cards, and rinsed-out soft drink cans. You may want to keep some extra items on hand for students who forget to bring something.

2. Model how to share: "I chose this water bottle. I think it will last one hundred years in a landfill because it's made of plastic. I see a lot of people drinking water from bottles like these when I go to the gym." Tell students that if they disagree with someone's prediction of what will be in the landfill in one hundred years, they should hold their thoughts because they'll have time for discussion later in the day.

3. Going around the circle, each student shares their item. As students share, you can list items or put them all in a bin for later use.

4. Give students time later to share their thoughts about the items that will be in the landfill. They can also discuss how to make a more sustainable choice for each item rather than adding it to the landfill, such as using a reusable bottle for water.

Group Activity

Building Whole-Class Identity

A third grade class is intent on guessing a category made up by their classmate, Caleb, who is doling out indirect clues in a game called Aunt Minerva (page 124).

"Aunt Minerva likes Florida but doesn't like Alaska," announces Caleb.

No responses.

Caleb tries again. "Aunt Minerva likes heavy down blankets but doesn't like thin sheets."

Two hands shoot up, and Caleb calls on Sonya.

"Aunt Minerva likes soup but doesn't like ice cream?" ventures Sonya, her voice making the statement a question.

"That's true," nods Caleb. "Danny?"

Danny has retracted his hand after hearing Sonya's contribution. "Nope, I'm not ready yet."

After a few more guesses about Aunt Minerva's preferences, half the hands in the circle are raised, and Mr. Bergstrom, the teacher, spots a good stopping place. All have grappled with the process of set-making that's integral to this game, and Mr. Bergstrom knows it's important to stop while students are still engaged with the activity.

"Pick a guesser, Caleb," Mr. Bergstrom directs, and Caleb points to Josie.

"Is it hot and cold?" she asks.

Caleb's smile and nod confirm it.

Meanwhile, down the hall, a fifth grade class is doing the Beach Ball activity (page 125) to practice finding the least common multiple of two numbers, something the class is working on. Most students figure out their answer with relative ease; a few lean to a neighbor for help.

And downstairs in a first grade classroom, a chorus of six- and seven-year-old voices offers up a singsong rendition of "My Bonnie" (page 132). "We've got the words down," says their teacher. "Now, when you sing a word that starts with B, stand up, and on the next B word, sit back down. Keep doing that throughout the whole song."

Eyes twinkle as the children await their teacher's signal to begin. The song begins again, and children pop up and drop back down in rapid succession. As they finish, they break into grins and delighted laughter.

Their teacher offers a compliment: "Great job, everyone! You all stayed in control of your voices and bodies, and that helped us all enjoy the activity."

Overview

As the above vignettes illustrate, group activities are short and fast-paced and involve everyone in the class participating at their own level. Through the activity, the teacher and students together build a repertoire of physical, intellectual, or artistic activities that may include active games, math activities, choral and poetry readings, memorization, singing, and chanting. Though they may appear to be just for fun, they support crucial learning goals: some activities incorporate academic skill-building components that tie in to current topics in the curriculum; others offer practice in important generalized skills like listening, following directions, exercising self-control, or practicing deductive reasoning. Regardless of the nature of the activities, they all contribute to a valuable aspect of optimal learning conditions: a positive classroom community.

Purposes and Goals of Group Activity

Group activities share five common purposes that are explored in the following sections.

Goals of Group Activity

- Contribute to the class's sense of community and group identity by building a repertoire of common songs, games, chants, and poems.

- Foster active and engaged participation.

- Encourage inclusion and cooperation.

- Help students learn the value of persistence and practice.

- Strengthen academic and social skills.

Group Activity Contributes to the Class's Sense of Community and Group Identity

It's cleanup time, and Shawna and Leo are methodically taking the large wooden unit blocks from their skyscraper and stacking them neatly on the appointed shelf. "My Bonnie lies over the ocean," sings Leo under his breath as he leans from the pile of blocks to the shelf, lost in his rhythm of stacking and tidying. "My Bonnie lies over the sea," Shawna chimes in. Her voice layers over her companion's as neatly as the blocks they stack on the shelf.

The chants and songs, games and storylines introduced during group activity time are a common and important currency in the learning community. They contribute to a shared archive from which students can draw, whether during a companionable cleanup moment, on a field trip bus ride, or at the lunch table. We feel a sense of belonging, comfort, and acceptance when we recognize a familiar melody, when we are invited into a game and realize that we know the rules, or when someone refers to a funny story and we find that we know that story, too. We are at home in this place with these people.

Sometimes the common learning gives us a way to affirm our group identity within a larger community. When a first grade class stands before the rest of the school and sings a song they've learned as a cohesive group, it's a wonderful declaration of their solidarity.

Group Activity Fosters Active and Engaged Participation

Good choices for group activities are engaging rather than passive and require everyone's participation. They can be a great boost at the start of the day because they demand that each of us pays attention and contributes. It's not easy to snooze through a fast-paced game of Zoom (page 137). And you need to pay attention when your turn to think up an equation for today's date is coming soon and the first six people have used up the obvious number statements.

Joining the tempo of a well-chosen group activity can help students find a productive pace for moving into the rest of the day. As individuals, we all have different rhythms and gaits, and our

differences bring richness to the group. We also have days when our pace is off. Students may come to school distracted, replaying a breakfast table argument with a sibling. Or they may arrive frazzled, rushing to compensate for oversleeping, needing help to change gears and settle down. Joining a group activity, moving in unison, enables students to focus and find a comfortable stride.

Group Activity Encourages Inclusion and Cooperation

Good group activities allow all members to take part. Although some students will excel in certain activities and some in others, each group activity must be accessible to all and allow everyone to begin the day with a sense of success. A teacher's knowledge of their class will guide the choice of activities. They shouldn't all feel easy—a sure route to complaints of "boring." But neither should they be ones in which only a couple of "gifted" students can feel successful; that will demoralize and isolate the rest of the group. Celebrating individual talents and achievements is healthy in a classroom, but group activity is not the place for it.

Group activities should be cooperative, not competitive, in nature. If you occasionally want to introduce an element of competition, try having the group compete against itself. Can they beat their previous time at Telegraph (page 136), a game in which they must work together to pass a hand squeeze around the circle as quickly as possible? Can they come up with more equations that equal twenty-three on the twenty-third of this month than they could on the twenty-third of last month? Many classes enjoy keeping a log of their best times for various activities. But even this kind of competition is best used sparingly so that the emphasis remains on the activity rather than the contest.

Browse the Group Activity Ideas section on page 122 as you get started!

Group Activity Helps Students Learn the Value of Persistence and Practice

Successful activities can stretch the group in positive ways. Helping the class to notice their increasing proficiency with a challenging activity affirms the role of practice and persistence in learning. But the challenges need to be deliberate choices on the teacher's part. They must first be sure that a sufficient level of safety has developed within the group, and then choose activities that highlight the whole group's growth rather than that of individuals.

A group of fifth graders once groaned, upon a first read-through of the Gettysburg Address during social studies, "We'll never be able to say this! We can't even pronounce half these words." And they were right. They couldn't pronounce them. Over the following two weeks, the class used Morning Meeting time to supplement their learning of the speech. During group activity, the teacher coached and students practiced. At the end of those two weeks, these fifth graders could do more than pronounce. They proclaimed—with resonant voices and not a single stumble.

"Remember how two weeks ago you thought you were never going to be able to recite this?" their teacher reminded them. This is such an important lesson: what seems insurmountable at first can indeed be surmounted with effort and support. Learning this lesson will serve these students well as they go on to confront the mysteries of algebra or the unfamiliar constructions of a new language.

Group Activity Strengthens Academic and Social Skills

Group activity abounds with opportunities to integrate the academic curriculum. In addition, because the activities are interactive, they also teach and reinforce social skills. However, to ensure that all students start their day with a sense of accomplishment and a reminder that they are successful learners, Morning Meeting group activities are designed to enable students to practice, apply, or extend familiar skills and concepts. The introduction of new material is best saved for specific instructional periods.

Many games lend themselves to the incorporation of academic material such as content area vocabulary or math skills practice. Even when games don't directly incorporate curriculum content, they teach skills that are important to academic success: observing, focusing, collaborating, thinking creatively, problem-solving.

And group activities don't have to be games. A successful activity might be a group recitation of a poem. It might be a round of group story-writing with an emphasis on trying varied sentence structures, or a chant with repeating phrases that reinforce pattern recognition. All these pursuits can be highly engaging for students while strengthening their academic and social skills.

Getting Started

Consider the following advice as you introduce group activity and try out new ideas with the class.

Model Appropriate Behaviors When Introducing Group Activity

Just as with all classroom activities, how a teacher introduces Morning Meeting group activity has a significant effect on students' success with it. Explain that this is a time within Morning Meeting when the whole group will do an activity together. In whatever language is appropriate and respectful to the age group, note that it will be important in these activities for each person to take good care of themselves as well as other people in the group. It often works well to begin by saying something like, "The third part of our Morning Meeting each day will be an activity that we'll do together as a whole group. We'll be moving, talking, acting, singing, chanting, or playing a game. As we do all these active things, what will we need to remember to do so that all of us can enjoy this time and learn together?"

After students share some ideas, choose a couple that are important to the activity for the day and model constructive behaviors related to those ideas. Eventually, you'll find it helpful to model the following:

- How to move safely through the circle

- How to keep your body in control

- How to wait for your turn

- What to do if someone makes a mistake

- What voice level to use (for speaking, chanting, and singing)

- What to do if a classmate needs help

- How to help everyone feel included

- How to work with a partner or small group

Eventually is a key word here. Opportunities to model activities and discuss how they're going will happen throughout the year. Carefully choose relatively simple, low-risk activities at the outset so that the group experiences success without the need for extensive preparation. Modeling one element at a time, specifically and thoroughly, works better than trying to conduct an exhaustive grand tour of constructive activity behaviors.

Also, spend some time thinking about what academic skills the class might need to learn or review for a group activity you're planning, and then teach the skills one at a time so students have a scaffold for achieving success. As the class is ready, you can add variations to the activity or introduce new, more complex activities.

For younger children, consider teaching complex activities over several days. For example, for songs, chants, and poems, start by having children simply echo each line as you read it. On another day, have the class sing or recite the lines chorally without echoing you. Still later, add movements for each line.

For older students, you can often similarly break down complex activities but cover all the steps in the same meeting. For example, the first time students do What Are You Doing? (page 137), a pantomime activity in which two students at a time interact in the center of the circle, you might model how to move safely into and out of the center, how to do the pantomime, and how to interact respectfully.

Interactive Modeling is an effective way to teach or review skills students need for a group activity. "Today we're going to play a fast and in-control game of Speed Ball" (page 135), Mr. Coughlin tells his first grade class. "I'm going to throw the ball to Willy. Watch and tell me what makes my throw both fast and in control." He throws the ball low and carefully, and Willy catches it easily.

> "What did you notice that made that throw both fast and in control?"
>
> "You didn't wing it at him," volunteers Zeke.
>
> "That's right. And where did I aim it?"
>
> "At his belly."
>
> Mr. Coughlin nods.
>
> "You threw it kind of easy," offers Claire.
>
> "Why did I do that? Wouldn't it be faster to throw it hard?"
>
> "No," maintains Claire. "Because Willy's not that far away from you and it would probably just bounce off him, or it would go out of the circle and he would have to go get it, and then it would really slow things down."

Aaron's hand is up. He is a versatile and talented athlete and loves any chance to throw a ball—or talk about it. "If you were throwing at Amy or somebody all the way across the circle, you'd have to throw harder, though."

"So you noticed," summarizes Mr. Coughlin, naming specific behaviors with key words that can be quick reminders later, "that I used careful aim and a just-hard-enough throw, depending on whom I'm throwing to."

He then invites a student volunteer to demonstrate a throw using those behaviors. Finally, Mr. Coughlin has the class practice briefly before beginning the Speed Ball activity "for real." The modeling takes only a few minutes, and Mr. Coughlin offers a chance for students to try applying the behaviors right away—an important step in helping students truly absorb new learning.

Model How to Handle Mistakes

Fourth grade teacher Mr. Roth is determined that his classroom will be one in which making a mistake is fine for any student—during group activity or any other time of day. He conveys this message daily in various ways, from displaying a poster on the wall that says "The only person who doesn't make a mistake is a person who never does anything," to telling stories from his own everyday life that feature an error in thinking and the learning he gained from it. It is not a message accepted readily by nine-year-olds, who are painfully aware and critical of their own and their peers' imperfections, so when Mr. Roth introduces a new group activity in which students create equations, he helps them learn how to respond when mistakes are made.

"When we do an activity like this, we will sometimes make mistakes," he says. "It's important that we notice mistakes in an honest and respectful way so that we can learn from them."

Earlier he had enlisted Jocelyn, a student for whom math comes easily, to help with today's modeling. Now he brings her into the lesson: "Today is the fourth. Jocelyn, please use the number four to make up an equation that has a mistake in it. I'm going to be a student who catches the mistake. Everyone, watch me and notice how I respond."

> "One hundred divided by twenty is four," offers Jocelyn, writing it on the chart.
>
> Mr. Roth looks thoughtful for a moment and then slowly puts his hand up. "I think that one hundred divided by twenty is five."
>
> Breaking out of acting mode, he turns to the class and asks, "What did you notice?"
>
> Kelly responds first: "You didn't shoot your hand up really fast, like, 'Ooh, ooh, I see a mistake!'"
>
> "What did I do?" asks Mr. Roth.
>
> "You put it up like normal—it wasn't a big deal," Kelly adds, and other students chime in.
>
> "You kept your voice nice and didn't sound like a know-it-all."
>
> "You said what you thought was right, not that Jocelyn was wrong."
>
> "You didn't laugh or roll your eyes."
>
> "What did my face look like?" inquires Mr. Roth.
>
> "You had your regular face on."

As the modeling ends and flows seamlessly into the activity, Mr. Roth watches for students putting their newly learned skill into action when classmates make mistakes.

Reflecting on the lesson later, he's pleased that the students recognized the details of what makes for an honest and respectful response to a mistake. He also knows that habits don't change easily and that in the days and weeks ahead, eyes will roll and hands will wave excitedly at a mistake. And he will remind, redirect, and reinforce— always with the same respect he has asked students to show when they notice others' mistakes.

Choose Activities That Fit the Group at This Particular Time

Group activities can vary widely. Some involve movement and others are more stationary; some are playful, others serious; many draw on the curriculum; some are brainteasers, while others tap students' artistic side. Choosing activities highlights the teacher's role as balance-keeper and knower-of-the-group. Students' maturity levels, their experience with doing group activities, their academic and social skill levels, the season of the school year, the group's degree of cohesiveness, and its temperament are all factors in determining which activities will be most beneficial.

Is it the beginning of the year, before students even know each other's names? If so, naming, introduction, or interview activities tend to work well. Midyear, when the class has begun to build trust and is developing a repertoire of academic and social skills, you might choose more complex or curriculum-based activities.

Is this a serious group that could use some lightening up? Perhaps Zoom (page 137) or Zip, Zap, Pop (page 137) would be just the thing. Or do you have a class of students who lack confidence in academics? Memorizing a serious and beautiful poem together may help them look at themselves differently.

In upper grades, you will want to pay particular attention to students' developmental needs. Older students who are conscious of leaving childhood behind and eager to be considered more adult might benefit from an activity such as Pica Ferme Nada (page 134), which requires increased skill and self-control. But they may also be delighted to engage in a familiar childhood game like Find the Leader (page 128) and relish the opportunity to regress for a few minutes.

Keep in mind that throughout the year you can adjust any activity to meet the developmental needs, abilities, and mood of the students you're teaching to best support their learning and growth. As you look at a particular activity, consider how you might adapt it to incorporate aspects of your specific academic curriculum. Also ask yourself how you might adapt it to accommodate a group that is:

- Shy, nervous, or reluctant to participate

- Rowdy and silly

- Still gaining all the knowledge and skills needed to participate successfully

Finally, consider shifting to students some of the responsibility for making activities work. Many teachers, after introducing a new activity, ask the group some reflective questions:

- What made it work?

- What made it engaging?

- What could we do next time to make it even more successful?

This gets students thinking about how they work together and increases their investment.

Look to Academics for Activity Ideas

Keep in mind that coming up with group activity ideas needn't be one more thing to add on to your busy day; instead, they can spring from the content you're already teaching.

Picture these scenes. A group of fifth graders, totally involved, mentally wrestle together with a tricky logic problem drawn from their math unit. Down the hall, third graders clap out the syllables in their weekly list of spelling words, feet tapping along. In a first grade room, the class is proudly reading in unison a poem hand-lettered in large print on an easel in the circle. In another primary class, students are using their bodies to make a beaver lodge and act out the activities of a beaver colony, representing and extending the learning they have gained from their study of beavers.

Each of these activities comes straight from the class's curriculum and meets the criteria for group activity perfectly: they are noncompetitive and inclusive, they require attention and alertness; they build the group's sense of how they can problem-solve together, and they develop a group voice, intelligence, and identity.

When you're looking for activity ideas, think about your curriculum. Could students work through some math problems together? Play a word game that will build vocabulary? Construct a crossword puzzle that they post on the school website? Could you find a poem about rivers that would tie in to the week's geography focus and make a great choral reading?

Group activity time might also be the perfect opportunity for a structured discussion. In addition to allowing students to share information about themselves, Inside-Outside Circles (page 97) can be used to talk about academic topics. Pose an open-ended question (one that has many possible reasonable answers) drawn from the curriculum—perhaps "Why do you think the protagonist in our story went against the wishes of his team?" or "Which historical figure from the civil rights movement would you like to meet and why?" After several rounds, a few students share with the whole group some of the ideas they heard. Again, the activity is inclusive, enriching, and engaging, and it comes right out of the class's academic work.

Understand Group Activity Responsibilities

In implementing and assessing group activity, keep the following general responsibilities in mind.

Teacher's responsibilities:

- Choose a variety of age-appropriate activities that include all skill levels.

- Make sure many different kinds of activities are represented—songs, poems, games, chants, movement, and so on—and that children have a chance to be physical, intellectual, artistic, playful, and serious.

- Give directions that are simple, clear, and consistent.

- Make sure everyone knows the rules for each activity.

- Model and practice skills that children need to be successful.

- Select activities that are inclusive of all and cooperative rather than competitive in nature.

- Model being playful and enthusiastic without being silly.

- Stop the activity and regroup if it's not going well.

- Reflect with students when necessary to make the next group activity more successful.

Students' responsibilities:

- Participate fully in all activities.

- Interact with all classmates.

- Show respect and support for the efforts of all participants.

- Have fun without being silly.

- Keep bodies and voice level in control.

- Work hard without being competitive.

- Follow the rules of activities.

Common Questions

Q What do I need to keep in mind as I plan group activities to ensure they are inclusive for all?

A Keeping the needs of all learners in mind while planning group activities is essential. Whether accommodations need to be made for students with physical, verbal, social, emotional, cognitive, or academic limitations, the important thing is to ensure the group activity allows all members to be part of the experience. For example, limited English speakers and nonverbal students can be supported with simple language and physical or picture cues. During a game of Zoom, students might have the option of saying the words or displaying one of two sides of a card, one side with Zoom and the other with Eek. Offer these accommodations to all students and not simply the student needing the assistance. And always consider comfort levels. Whether a student is from a culture that restricts physical contact with people outside the family or a student simply does not feel comfortable with physical interaction, honor their choice. Choose activities (especially at the start of the year) that do not involve touching classmates. As the year progresses, you can institute a "challenge by choice" and provide the entire class with alternatives if and when activities for physical interaction are introduced.

Often, a simple variation in an activity can make it more inclusive for your group. Here are some examples:

- **Beach Ball** (page 125), with the vocabulary variation, can be modified to support students with verbal or cognitive limitations by placing a picture sticker instead of a word in each section of the ball. Also, students can simply name the item pictured and use it in a sentence without giving a definition of the item.

- **Cooper Says** (page 126), with instructions that vary depending on physical limitations. For example, if a student has limited use of their lower body, the instructions might focus on upper body movements, such as "Close your eyes. Touch your nose. Raise your right arm."

- **Near and Far**. In this variation of Hot and Cold (page 130), classmates give the seeker distance clues, such as "You're getting nearer . . . you're very near it," or "You're far away," instead of "hot" and "cold," which, used in this manner, could confuse students beginning to learn English.

Q I know that activities should be engaging and enjoyable, but my class gets really silly and doesn't take them seriously. Any suggestions?

A You're right to draw a distinction between enjoying something and being silly. Whereas enjoyment can enhance learning, silliness is distracting and gets in the way of group engagement. Monitoring the tone is an important teacher job in Morning Meeting. Give a reminder at the first sign of silliness, before that tone takes hold.

Sometimes students need more than a reminder. Observe to see where the silliness is coming from. If it's one or two students, directing them to go to positive time-out often works to stop the behavior and keep the silliness from spreading. Also, consider whether something about the particular activity is making it hard for those students to join in wholeheartedly. You may need to speak to them individually to say what you notice and ask them to think of ways they can help group activity work better.

When the silliness is group-wide, you may sometimes need to call a class time-out and lead the group in reflecting on what is going on so you can come up with possible solutions. Maybe a change in the activities themselves is in order. Perhaps it's time to switch for a while to very structured activities that offer greater challenge and help the group take itself more seriously.

Don't be afraid to stop an activity that feels too silly so you can take corrective action. And remember the importance of responding immediately, when the behavior is still minor, to keep things from getting out of hand.

Q **The same students always seem to "star" in group activity. How can I address this?**

A One important way is to make sure the activities are varied, calling upon many different modes of communication and interaction. We all have different areas in which we shine and in which we struggle. Some of us are graceful and coordinated, while some are verbally quick and playful. Some have terrific recall and excel at memory games and recitation, while others are theatrical and can pantomime any emotion down to its every nuance. Still others have a gift of melody that enables a class to sound beautiful when they sing together.

Making sure our activities engage many different aptitudes ensures that all students will have a chance to shine—and not shine. Anyone may sometimes feel a little foolish; all will often feel smart. In time, students learn they can participate even if they don't excel at the activity of the moment. Marisol learns that when she stands next to Casey she can, in fact, carry a tune. Wesley learns that if he forgets a line in the skit, he can glance at Habiba, who will remember and give him a cue.

Q **One of the students in this year's class hangs back and is very reluctant to participate in group activity. How can I encourage this child to join in?**

A This is a situation in which a teacher's knowledge of individual students is crucial. What does this student choose to do at recess or choice times? What are their areas of comfort and skill? Suppose the student is like Giselle, who excels at anything with the suffix -ball. Then you could choose some activities involving ball-throwing. If the student is like Steven, who has a wealth of information about the latest world conflict or most recent movie blockbuster, you could structure some activities around current events or popular culture.

Another possibility with a shy or reticent student: if you're teaching the group a new activity, you might elicit this student's help ahead of time to try it out and coteach it to the group with you.

Group Activity Ideas

As with the other components of Morning Meeting, choose a group activity that meets the needs of the day, students' developmental levels, and students' comfort with one another.

Group Activity for:

 Beginning of Year

 Later in Year

 Younger Grades

 Older Grades

 Academic Content Reinforcement

 Songs, Chants, and Movements

Group Activity	PAGE	Beginning of Year	Later in Year	Younger Grades	Older Grades	Academic Content	Songs, Chants, Movements
Alibi	123		✓		✓		
Alphabet Story	123		✓	✓	✓	✓	
Aroostasha	124	✓		✓	✓		✓
Aunt Minerva	124		✓		✓	✓	
Beach Ball	125		✓	✓	✓	✓	
Category Snap	125		✓	✓	✓	✓	✓
Clapping Names	126	✓		✓			✓
Cooper Says	126	✓		✓	✓		
Day at the Museum	127		✓	✓	✓		
Do What I Said Not What I Say	127		✓	✓	✓		✓
Famous Pairs	128		✓		✓	✓	
Find the Leader	128	✓		✓	✓		
Guess the Number	129		✓	✓	✓	✓	
Hands Up for '23	129		✓		✓	✓	✓
Hot and Cold	130	✓		✓	✓		
Human Protractor	130		✓	✓	✓	✓	
I Sit in the Grass	131		✓		✓		
Incorporations	131		✓	✓	✓		
Mental Math Push-Ups	132		✓		✓	✓	
My Bonnie	132	✓		✓			✓
Mystery Word	133		✓	✓	✓		
Nonverbal Birthday Lineup	133	✓			✓		
Oliver Twist	133	✓		✓			✓
One Thing You Like to Do	134	✓		✓	✓		✓
Pica Ferme Nada	134		✓		✓	✓	
Scientific Pros and Cons	135		✓		✓	✓	
Speed Ball	135		✓	✓	✓		
Take Sides	135	✓		✓	✓		
Telegraph	136		✓	✓	✓		
A Warm Wind Blows	136	✓		✓	✓		
What Are You Doing?	137		✓	✓	✓		✓
Zip, Zap, Pop	137		✓	✓	✓		
Zoom	137		✓	✓	✓		

Alibi

1. Choose a student to be the detective and have them leave the room.

2. While the detective is gone, the group chooses one person to be the gremlin and another to be the spokesperson. Everyone else is a suspect.

3. The gremlin changes something obvious in the room, such as moving the hamster's cage. The gremlin and the suspects all make up one-sentence alibis (for example, "I never moved from this spot!").

4. The detective returns to the circle, and the spokesperson tells them what has changed.

5. Going around the circle, the detective asks each student, "Where were you when [the hamster's cage was moved]?" Students state their alibis.

6. The detective now goes around the circle a second time, again asking for alibis. Everyone but the gremlin restates their original alibi—the gremlin changes their alibi slightly. The detective then has three guesses to discover the gremlin. If they don't guess correctly, the gremlin says, "I did it!"

Variation: To make this activity more challenging, students could add more details to their alibis, or all students except the gremlin could change their alibis.

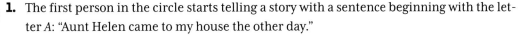

Alphabet Story

1. The first person in the circle starts telling a story with a sentence beginning with the letter *A*: "Aunt Helen came to my house the other day."

2. The next person in the circle continues, adding a sentence that begins with *B*: "Buddy, her terrier, came with her."

3. The class continues through the alphabet until everyone has added to the story.

Group Activity for:

 Beginning of Year

 Later in Year

 Younger Grades

 Older Grades

 Academic Content Reinforcement

 Songs, Chants, and Movements

Aroostasha

1. Students stand in a circle with their hands clasped in front of them, fingers interlaced.

2. Begin the activity by demonstrating the chant and body movements. Chant, "Aroostasha, aroostasha, aroostasha-sha," while gradually moving your clasped hands across your body from right to left and pulsing them up and down to the beat. Repeat, moving your hands gradually back to the right side of your body.

3. Have the class repeat the chant and body movements after you.

4. Do additional rounds, calling out a new body position to add in each time, such as:

   - Thumbs up

   - Wrists together

   - Elbows in

   - Knees together

   - Toes in

   - Bottom out

   - Tongue out (Ever try to say "Aroostasha" with your tongue out? Kids really get a laugh out of this!)

Aunt Minerva

1. The student who starts the activity decides on a category but doesn't tell anyone. Instead, they hint at the category by naming things that Aunt Minerva likes and doesn't like. For example, if the category is "high and low," they might say, "Aunt Minerva likes mountains but doesn't like oceans. Aunt Minerva likes birds' nests but doesn't like rabbit holes."

2. The other students try to figure out the category based on the clues. When a student thinks they know the category, they raise their hand.

3. The starter calls on one classmate at a time to guess. That classmate gives an example of their own without naming the category: "Aunt Minerva likes clouds but doesn't like grass."

4. The starter acknowledges whether the statement is true and continues giving examples to help more classmates figure out the category.

5. Once a solid number (perhaps half) of students have their hands raised to guess, have the starter reveal the category.

6. Choose another student to begin a new round.

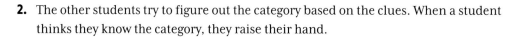

Beach Ball

1. Before doing the activity, write a number on each panel of a beach ball and the small circles at the top and bottom of the ball.

2. Begin by announcing a math function, such as addition, subtraction, multiplication, or division, and then tossing the ball to someone in the circle.

3. The person who catches the ball looks at the numbers beneath or near their hands. These numbers become an equation that the student tries to solve using the designated function. For example, if the function is multiplication and the student's hands cover a three and a seven, they need to multiply three times seven and give the correct answer. The student can ask for help if needed.

4. Once the equation is solved, the student tosses the ball to someone else in the group.

Variation: You can adapt this activity for many subject areas. For example, instead of numbers, write vocabulary words on each panel of a beach ball. The student who catches the ball defines one of the words near where their hands are and uses it in a sentence. (If you have students who are beginning readers or who are just learning English, you can vary this activity by placing picture stickers on each panel. The student who catches the ball looks at the stickers under or near their hands. They name one of the items and then use that word in a sentence.)

Category Snap

1. The group sits in a circle. Choose one person to be the leader.

2. The leader starts a rhythm using a sequence of knee slap, hand clap, right-hand finger snap, left-hand finger snap.

3. Once the rhythm is established, the leader announces a category, such as fruits, on the right-hand finger snap and names an example, such as apples, with the left-hand finger snap.

4. The next person in the circle repeats "apples" with the right-hand finger snap and then a new example in that same category with the left-hand finger snap: Knee slap, hand clap, "apples, apricots."

5. The play continues around the circle with each person repeating the previous person's example on the right snap and naming their own on the left snap. Once an item has been named, it cannot be used again.

Group Activity for:

  Beginning of Year

 Later in Year

 Younger Grades

 Older Grades

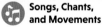 **Academic Content Reinforcement**

Songs, Chants, and Movements

Variation: Announce the category before the activity begins. Give students a moment to think of several examples of that category, and let students know that they'll need to pay attention and remember what each class-mate says. Then, going around the circle, each person names an item with no repetitions. Once everyone has named an item, the leader begins the knee slap, hand clap, finger snap rhythm. With the right-hand finger snap, they name their own item, and with the left-hand finger snap, they name another student's item. That student then names their own item and another student's item, and so on. This variation sends the action jumping around the circle.

Clapping Names

1. This is a good activity to do at the beginning of the year when children are learning each other's names. It's also good to do if a new child joins the class later in the year.

2. Explain that the class will clap out the number of syllables in each person's first name while they chant the name.

3. You can begin with yourself: say your name, then have the whole class repeat it while clapping on each syllable.

4. Either go around the room or ask children to volunteer to be next.

Variation: Once the class is familiar with everyone's first name, try having them clap out last names or self-chosen nicknames.

Cooper Says

1. This activity is similar to Simon Says, except that no one is ever "out."

2. Choose someone to be the leader, "Cooper," to give the group instructions.

3. Students follow the instructions only if the instructions are preceded by "Cooper says . . ." For example, if the leader says, "Cooper says touch your toes," students touch their toes. However, if the leader says, "Touch your toes," students stand still.

4. Keep the activity moving quickly. You can increase the difficulty by challenging the group to follow ten directions correctly.

Day at the Museum

1. To begin, one person is appointed "guard," and the rest of the players are appointed "statues."

2. The guard stands at the edge of the group and turns their back. While their back is turned, the statues come to life and move and dance around silently.

3. When the guard turns around, all of the statues have to freeze.

4. If the guard catches a player moving, they become a "permanent seated statue" and are out.

5. Play continues until one statue is left. That statue becomes the next guard.

Variation: Teachers could take on the role of "guard" or give a specific movement for statues to perform to make the activity more low risk for students.

Do What I Said Not What I Say

Stand facing the children and call out a command. Students must follow the previously given command, not the immediate one. For example:

Leader: Stand on one foot!
(Students do nothing.)

Leader: Hop on one foot!
(Students stand on one foot.)

Leader: Flap your arms!
(Students hop on one foot.)

Leader: Pat your head!
(Students flap their arms.)

Leader: Sit down!
(Students pat their heads.)

Leader: Fold your hands on your desks!
(Students sit down.)

Leader: Fold your hands on your desks!
(Students fold their hands on their desks and are ready for the next lesson or activity of the day.)

Scan the QR code to see this activity in action.

Variation: To add more challenge, the leader may pantomime the motion as well as say it.

Famous Pairs

Group Activity for:

 Beginning of Year

 Later in Year

 Younger Grades

 Older Grades

 Academic Content Reinforcement

Songs, Chants, and Movements

1. Make a list of famous pairs of people with whom the class is familiar, such as Lewis and Clark or Watson and Crick. You could brainstorm a list with the class. Write these names on cards, one name to a card.

2. Shuffle the cards, and then tape one to each student's back.

3. Students mill around, asking each other questions to determine what name is on their back.

4. Everyone then finds the person who has their partner's name.

5. Pairs return to the circle, standing or sitting next to each other.

Find the Leader

1. Designate one student to be the guesser. They go and stand someplace where they cannot see the group.

2. Say, "Raise your hand if you would like to be the leader." Without speaking, choose a leader from the volunteers.

3. The leader begins doing a motion, such as tapping their hands against their knees. Going around the circle, the rest of the class mimics that motion. The leader then does a different motion, which proceeds around the circle until everyone has switched.

4. The guesser comes back to the circle and stands in the middle. They look around and try to guess who the leader is.

5. If they don't guess correctly after three tries, reveal the leader to limit frustration and keep the activity positive. As time allows, do additional rounds with new guessers and leaders.

Variations:

*   Have more than one guesser and have them confer before guessing.

*   Have two leaders take turns starting new movements. The guesser tries to identify both leaders.

*   Limit movements to those that are silent to increase the challenge.

Guess the Number

1. Tell the class you've chosen a number between one and ____, naming a range that's appropriately challenging for the age and skill level of the group.

2. Going around the circle, students ask yes-or-no questions to try to determine the number (or say "Pass" if they'd like). Encourage students to think of questions that will give them information about the number, rather than questions that just eliminate one number. For example, instead of asking if it's the number after fourteen, students might ask if it's a two-digit number, whether it's greater than ten, or if it has a five in it.

3. Anyone can try to guess the number at any time. If the guess is incorrect, the questioning continues.

4. If the guess is correct, start another round by choosing or having a student choose another number. To emphasize collaboration rather than competition, be sure the new number chooser isn't the person who guessed correctly in the previous round.

Hands Up for '23

1. Name an academic category (for example, capital cities) and choose a student to go first in naming something in that category.

2. The group begins the following chant, filling in the name of the category in line four.

Hands up	(raise both hands)
For '23	(change to current year)
Gonna name	(clap, clap)
Some [category]	(clap, clap)
One apiece	(clap, clap)
No repeats	(clap, clap)
No hesitation	(clap, clap)
No duplication	(clap, clap)
Starting with	(clap, clap)
[Student's name]	(clap, clap)

3. The last line of the chant names the person who goes first. That person says an item in the category; then, going quickly around the circle, each person names a different item in the category. For example:

Sacramento	(clap, clap)
Boston	(clap, clap)
Austin	(clap, clap)

4. Continue all the way around the circle. Repeat with new categories as time allows, starting with a different student each time.

Group Activity for:

 Beginning of Year

 Later in Year

 Younger Grades

 Older Grades

 Academic Content Reinforcement

Songs, Chants, and Movements

Hot and Cold

1. Select an object to hide.

2. Choose one student to be the seeker and send them out of the room.

3. Hide the object in a place that is difficult enough to provide a challenge but not so difficult that the search becomes frustrating. The group can help you choose a good hiding place.

4. Invite the seeker back into the room.

5. The seeker begins looking for the object. The group guides the search by saying "Hot" whenever the seeker gets near the object and "Cold" whenever they move away from the object.

Variation: If you have students who are English language learners in the class who might be confused by using "hot" and "cold" in this way, you can use "near" and "far."

Human Protractor

1. Everyone stands in a circle, touching their toes.

2. Tell students they're going to straighten up gradually, keeping their arms stretched out in front of their bodies. At the same time, they'll be counting from zero to a number that you specify. By the time their hands are reaching overhead, they should be at the upper number. Let students know that they need to remember where their hands are at different numbers, and set the range of numbers to suit the age and abilities in your classroom (0–10, 0–100, 0–180, and so on; if counting to a higher number, you might have students count by fives or tens).

3. Once students have moved through the range of numbers from toes to overhead, call out numbers within the specified range.

4. Students take the position for each number as you call it.

5. When students are familiar with the activity, they can take turns being the number caller.

Variation: Students count from 0 to 100 percent as they move from touching toes to reaching overhead. Then, instead of calling out numbers, you could ask probability questions, such as "What is the likelihood of rain today?"

Variation: After students have moved through the number positions, have them do multiplication, addition, or subtraction problems that lead to an answer within the designated range. Each student does the calculation and then moves into the position for the answer. For example, if you called out, "Three times fifteen," they'd take the position for forty-five.

I Sit in the Grass

1. Create a circle of chairs that has one more chair than there are students participating. Students find places to sit, with one chair empty.

2. The student next to the empty chair is always the one to take action. The first student next to the empty spot says, "I sit," and slides over into the empty chair.

3. This opens up a new empty chair. The student next to that chair slides into it and says, "In the grass."

4. The student sitting next to the new empty chair slides over, saying, "With my friend."

5. The student next to the new empty chair slides over and says the name of someone else in the circle.

6. The student whose name was called gets up from their seat and goes to sit in that empty chair.

7. Now there is a new empty chair! The two students on either side of the open seat try to be the first to slide into that seat, which would make them the next student to start the activity.

8. Repeat steps 2–7 a few more times.

Variation: Consider writing the words of the chant so students can follow along and as a support.

Incorporations

1. Begin by ringing a chime or giving some other signal, and then give directions for forming groups, such as "Get into groups of three."

2. Students form groups as quickly as possible.

3. Once all students have formed groups of three, ring the chime again and give a different direction, such as "Get into groups where everyone is wearing something the same color."

4. Continue having students quickly form different groups for as long as time allows.

Mental Math Push-Ups

1. Write a series of math expressions on a whiteboard or chart (for example, 2 + 2 + 2, 3 + 3 – 3, 5 + 5 – 1). To help students focus, begin by covering up all the expressions except the first one.

2. Students work with a partner to find the answer to each expression in their head—no pencil or paper.

3. When you give the signal, all students give their answers at the same time.

4. Uncover each new expression as the rounds continue.

 Group Activity for:

 Beginning of Year

Later in Year

 Younger Grades

 Older Grades

 Academic Content Reinforcement

 **Songs, Chants, and Movements**

My Bonnie

1. Teach the class the song "My Bonnie Lies Over the Ocean." You may want to post the words where students can see them as they learn.

> My **B**onnie lies over the ocean.
> My **B**onnie lies over the sea.
> My **B**onnie lies over the ocean,
> Oh **b**ring **b**ack my **B**onnie to me.
> **B**ring **b**ack, **b**ring **b**ack,
> Oh **b**ring **b**ack my **B**onnie to me, to me.
> **B**ring **b**ack, **b**ring **b**ack,
> Oh **b**ring **b**ack my **B**onnie to me.

2. Once the class knows the tune, have them alternate between sitting and standing whenever words beginning with a *b* are sung. For example: "My Bonnie [stand] lies over the ocean. My Bonnie [sit] lies over the sea . . ."

Mystery Word

1. On index cards, write key vocabulary words from an article or topic students have been studying, one word per card.

2. Have students quickly summarize the article or topic and confirm that everyone is familiar with all the words written on the cards.

3. Choose a student to be the guesser and tape a word to their back. This student's job is to guess the word using clues from classmates. They move slowly around the inside of the circle, back turned to their classmates to let everyone else see the word.

4. The student calls on one classmate at a time to offer clues in the form of sentences that could include that word. For example, if students are studying environmental issues and the word is *extinct*, a clue might be "If sea ice keeps melting, polar bears might become blank."

5. The guesser guesses what the word is after each clue. If they get it right, another student takes a turn. If they have not guessed the word after three tries, the class reveals it to them.

Nonverbal Birthday Lineup

1. Have students line up according to their month and day of birth, without any talking. This challenges students to be inventive in communicating nonverbally. Remind children that they need to remain friendly and respectful as they use facial expressions and body language to communicate.

2. Once everyone is lined up, have them go down the line and say their birthday to see how accurate they were in communicating nonverbally.

Oliver Twist

1. The whole group recites the following chant and does the accompanying movements:

Oliver twist, twist, twist	(hands on hips and twist body)
Can't do this, this, this	(tap right foot and shake forefinger of right hand)
Touch his head, head, head	(touch head)
Touch his nose, nose, nose	(touch nose)
Touch his ears, ears, ears	(touch ears)
Touch his toes, toes, toes	(touch toes)

2. Repeat the chant several times, gradually speeding up until children are all laughing as they try to keep up.

One Thing You Like to Do

1. Let students know that they're each going to pantomime a favorite activity. Give them a minute to think of an activity and a simple movement they can do to represent that activity (for example, pretending to swing a baseball bat).

2. Going around the circle, each student does their movement, and classmates guess the activity. Remind students to wait until the pantomime is finished before they make their guesses.

Group Activity for:

 Beginning of Year

 Later in Year

 Younger Grades

 Older Grades

 Academic Content Reinforcement

 Songs, Chants, and Movements

Pica Ferme Nada

1. Begin by asking a student to think of a number with an agreed-upon number of digits (based on the age and skill level of the children playing). The student writes the number on a piece of paper, which they show to you and then put aside until the end of the activity.

2. On chart paper or the board, write a blank for each digit of the number. For example, write _ _ _ for a three-digit number.

3. Going around the circle, students try to figure out the number by suggesting three-digit numbers. For each suggestion, indicate how close it is to the mystery number using this code:

   Pica (P) means the numeral is in the mystery number but is in the wrong place.
   Ferme (F) means the numeral and place are correct.
   Nada (N) means the numeral is not in the mystery number at all.
   For example, if the mystery number is 386 and someone suggests 365, write "365 – F P N."

4. The next person in the circle suggests a number based on this information, asking classmates for help if they'd like. Continue around the circle with students making guesses. Anyone who wants to pass may do so.

5. The activity continues until someone is ready to name the number—and explain the thinking that solved the mystery.

Variation: Write the Pica, Ferme, and Nada symbols with no direct relationship to the placement of the numerals in the suggested number. For example, if the mystery number is 386 and a student suggests 365, you might write "N F P." If another student suggests 357, you might write "N F N." Students may welcome the extra challenge posed by the random placement of the symbols.

Scientific Pros and Cons

1. Students find a partner (or you assign partners).

2. Distribute a sheet of paper and a pencil to each pair.

3. Name a scientific venture they've been studying (such as bioengineering crops, introducing wolves or coyotes into an ecosystem to control the deer population, or using solar power) and let them know that they'll have a chance to think about the pros and cons of this venture.

4. Give partners one minute to list pros of the venture. Then ring a chime and have them list cons.

5. After a minute, ring the chime again and bring everyone back into the circle. Each pair then shares one pro and one con with the class.

Speed Ball

1. Have everyone sit or stand in a circle. Review safety parameters such as throwing under-hand, aiming toward the torso rather than the head, and keeping throws gentle.

2. Call out a student's name and quickly toss the ball to them.

3. That student catches it, holds it for just a second as they call out another student's name, tosses the ball to them, and puts a thumb up to indicate they've had a turn.

4. Continue in this way until everyone has had a chance to toss and to catch.

Take Sides

1. Make up a list of contrasting statements about students' preferences. For example: "I love to sleep late" and "I love to get up early," or "I like to be with big groups" and "I like to be with one friend."

2. With students standing in a line down the middle of the circle area, call out a pair of statements.

3. Students for whom the first statement is true take a step to the left; students for whom the second statement is true take a step to the right. Students who don't feel strongly about either statement stay where they are.

4. Continue calling out statements until everyone has moved a few times.

5. Finish with a statement that's true of everyone in the class: "If you're in the sixth grade, find a place to sit down in our circle."

Telegraph

1. Students stand in a circle, hold hands, and close their eyes.

2. The first student (or the teacher) chooses a nonverbal message, such as three quick, gentle hand squeezes, and sends it to the next child.

3. The child who received the message then sends it to the next person, and so on around the circle.

4. After the message goes around the whole circle, the last child explains verbally what it was.

Variation: Send the message in both directions at once until one child receives it from both sides.

 Beginning of Year

 Later in Year

 Younger Grades

Older Grades

Academic Content Reinforcement

Songs, Chants, and Movements

A Warm Wind Blows

1. Set up chairs in the meeting circle—one fewer than the number of people in the circle.

2. Everyone sits except for one person, who stands in the middle of the circle. They say, "A warm wind blows for anyone who _____," filling in the blank with a category (for example, "has a dog"). Encourage students to name categories that relate to interests, hobbies, and family rather than clothing or appearance. You could brainstorm a list of categories before beginning the activity.

3. Everyone who fits that category comes into the center of the circle and then quickly finds a new place to sit, including the student who started in the middle.

4. The one person who doesn't find a seat now stands in the center of the circle and says, "A warm wind blows for anyone who _____," naming a new category.

5. The activity continues for several rounds.

What Are You Doing?

1. A student goes to the center of the circle and pantomimes a simple action, such as brushing their hair.

2. The next student in the circle approaches the hair-brusher and asks, "What are you doing?"

3. The hair-brusher responds by saying something completely different, such as "I'm washing the floor," and then resumes their place in the circle.

4. The person who asked now pretends that they are washing the floor.

5. The next student in the circle approaches the floor-washer and asks, "What are you doing?"

6. This goes on until everyone in the circle has had a chance to pantomime an action.

Zip, Zap, Pop

1. A student begins by placing their right or left hand on top of their head so their fingers are pointing to the student on their right or left and saying "Zip."

2. The student who receives the zip can either pass it on to the next student in the circle or place their hand under their chin, pointing back toward the student who passed them the zip, and say, "Zap," or they can point at someone across the circle and say, "Pop."

3. Continue until everyone has been zipped, zapped, or popped.

Zoom

1. The person who begins the activity says, "Zoom!" and turns their head quickly to a neighbor on either the right or left.

2. That person passes the zoom to the next person, and so on around the circle.

3. You can challenge the group to go faster and use a stopwatch to time them.

Variation: Explain that the word "Eek!" stops the zoom and makes it reverse direction. For the next round, allow one eek, and then in subsequent rounds, increase the number of eeks allowed. Remind children that the goal is to get the zoom passed all the way around the circle. If only a few children have had a chance to say "Eek!" you can end the activity by having everyone say "Eek!" together.

Morning Message

A Letter to the Class

Our Class Name Chart

Abdirashid	Jailyne	Maria
Adoma	James	Pedro
Alayah	Terry	Rein
Almani	Joshua	Slava
Brithany	Joy	Sulaiman
Clemmie	Kenndolynn	Xianca
Elijah	Koah	Yakili
Hadeyf	Leah	Yaquelyn

Third grade teacher Ms. Alberti gets the class ready to read the morning message she has written to them. She divides the children into two groups and then directs their attention to the chart on an easel next to her. "We'll read alternate sentences by groups," she says. She points to the salutation. "Group one, you're on!"

When the students have read the entire message, Ms. Alberti reads the examples that students wrote on the chart before the meeting started: "Coffee, corn, popcorn, peanuts . . ."

She pauses and then asks, "What do you notice about the different seeds and foods made from seeds that we eat?"

"It's a long list," responds a student.

"Some we eat raw and some we eat cooked."

"We eat seeds all the time," another student says.

"You're right, we do," Ms. Alberti says. "Put your thumb up if you ate a seed or a seed food for breakfast." She pauses while thumbs go up. "Now, turn to your partner and brainstorm a list of seeds or foods made from seeds that are often breakfast foods."

A lively hum fills the room. After a few minutes, Ms. Alberti gets the students' attention. "Today, during lunch," she says, "notice if you're eating any seeds or foods made from seeds. This afternoon, during science, we'll add to our list."

Overview

Morning message provides information and academic reinforcement through a message written by the teacher each day. Students read the message as they enter the room and follow any instructions on it before Morning Meeting begins. Later, the message serves as the basis for the last component of Morning Meeting. During that component, teacher and students read the message, and the teacher engages the students in discussion based on its content.

Purposes and Goals of Morning Message

The content and format of the message change as children get older, and so do the ways in which students interact with the message before and during the meeting. The methods and purposes of morning message, however, stay the same. The three common purposes of morning messages are explored in the following sections.

> **Goals of Morning Message**
>
> • Build community through shared written information.
>
> • Develop and reinforce language arts, math, and other academic skills in a meaningful and interactive way.
>
> • Ease the transition into the rest of the day and build students' excitement about the day's learning.

Morning Message Builds Community Through Shared Written Information

Often, teachers write their messages in the form of a letter: "Dear Room 22 Students," "Good morning, Friendly Workers," "Hello, Multiplying Mathematicians!" the letters may begin. From the opening salutations, students are addressed as a group and reminded of their membership in the classroom community.

Each message focuses primarily on one topic, with content that is relevant to all students. As teachers compose their messages to the class, they consider students' development,

March 10

Hello, Botanists!

We have been learning about seeds. Did you know that we eat many different types of seeds and foods made from seeds?

In the space below, write a seed we eat or a food made from seeds. HINT: Look at the tray on the table.

Sincerely, Ms. Alberti

coffee

Popcorn Peanuts

CORN

skills, and interests, and what is happening in the classroom. Sometimes, as in the opening vignette, content is drawn from the academic curriculum; other times the message emphasizes social aspects of classroom life.

Sometimes students respond to a question in the message by writing or drawing right on the message. Other times students simply read and think about the message before the meeting. But no matter what the content and format, students begin their day engaging with a shared written communication in an inclusive experience—the message pertains to all, and we expect all to read and use it.

Morning Message Reinforces Language Arts, Math, and Other Academic Skills in a Meaningful and Interactive Way

The daily use of a written morning message provides an opportunity to practice a range of academic skills. For younger children, who are learning to read and write, the focus is often on literacy skills. The sentence structures and message formats are deliberately predictable and repetitious, and teachers include frequent picture cues and familiar sight vocabulary, with only the topic changing from day to day. "Today is Monday. We will paint," or "Today is November 16. We will count by twos in math." These simple sentence patterns, to which even the youngest quickly become accustomed, teach letter and number recognition, sight words, word families, and spelling and language patterns.

As students' abilities grow, teachers might include one or two sentences at the end of the message that use a new word or sentence structure, encouraging students to develop and practice strategies for independent reading of unfamiliar language. By looking to the day's activities or curriculum for the content of these sentences, teachers give children a taste of vocabulary they will see later in the day and help them transition into the day's learning: "We will use watercolors." "We will talk about our spider today."

Teachers may also include in their messages news or reminders about the day: "Bring your writing to Morning Meeting and be ready to share your opening sentence," "We have an assembly this afternoon," or "Chandra's dad will cook with us today." All children can benefit from this information, particularly students for whom predictability is especially important due to autism, toxic stress, or other circumstances.

During the morning message portion of Morning Meeting, the teacher asks questions or plays quick games based on the information on the chart. For example, a teacher in the younger grades might ask:

- Who can find the letter *t*?
- Who can find two letters that go together and make the sound "ba"?
- Who can make a number sentence for the number five?
- Who can name something in our room that we have five of?

For older students, morning messages may support more complex and varied content. Although morning messages are not intended for introducing new content or skills, they do offer many opportunities for older children to practice a range of academic skills they've been introduced to and are working on. Teachers will often include content-area vocabulary for review or provide models for the type of writing students will encounter in their reading. They might insert deliberate punctuation errors for students to find and fix or math problems to solve.

Often, teachers include an item that helps students learn about each other: "Who has a birthday this month?" "What's your favorite season?" "What book are you reading this week?" Teachers might include items that collect data about the class. For example, one message includes a chart listing sports (along with a "don't like any sport" column) and asks students to "Sign your name under your favorite sport." In the meeting itself, the class will discuss the data gathered and different ways they might graph it. Teachers may also take a moment to invite students who signed their name under "don't like any sport" to tell the class what nonsport hobby they like.

Highlights of Morning Message

- Includes a written message that welcomes and greets students as they enter the room

- Adds predictability and structure to morning arrival time

- Gets students excited about the day's learning

- Lets students know that the teacher has prepared for the day and is ready for them, which helps them feel safe and cared for

- Affords a fun and interactive way to review and practice reading, writing, math, and other skills

- Conveys that reading is a valuable way to get needed information

- Builds community through shared written information

- Provides a warm-up for the day's activities

- Eases the transition from Morning Meeting to the rest of the day

Morning Message Eases the Transition Into the Rest of the Day and Builds Excitement About the Day's Learning

Seeing an attractive and interesting message waiting at the beginning of the day is one way students know that their teacher is ready for them, has thought about the day, and is welcoming them to it. Of course, teachers use the message to supplement, rather than replace, greeting students and checking in with them face-to-face as they enter the classroom in the morning.

Not only does the message help welcome students to the classroom, but the information in the message prepares them for the day's learning and events and helps them reflect on the learning and events of previous days. The message draws students in as it invites them to begin participating even before Morning Meeting: "List one fact you know about Sojourner Truth." "Draw a food that you saw on our trip to the store yesterday." "Can you find a spelling mistake or two in this message?"

Browse the Morning Message Ideas section on page 154 as you get started!

During the morning message portion of Morning Meeting, the lively discussions and students' interaction with the message as a group help teachers send students into the rest of the day feeling engaged and capable, reassured about what they know and can do.

Getting Started

Here are some tips to keep in mind as you begin using morning messages.

Introduce Morning Message Slowly

As with other components of Morning Meeting, simplicity is best at first. Begin with simple messages and straightforward ways of reading them, and then slowly build challenge and complexity as students are ready. On the first day of school, you might have a welcoming message written and posted in the meeting circle. When you get to the morning message part of the meeting, point to the message and let students know that every day they will find a message from you that they should read before the meeting and that they will use during and after the meeting as well. Over the next few days, model and practice various ways of reading and interacting with the message when students arrive in the morning. It can be helpful to stand by the message chart during arrival time in the first week or so, greeting students and, if needed, providing some extra support in reading the message.

During those early days, when you get to the morning message portion of the meeting, you could read the message aloud with younger students, pointing to each word as you read. With older students, begin with choral reading for the first few days. When students are comfortable with choral reading, begin to vary the ways you read the message from day to day. For example, the class might echo you or a classmate line by line, different groups might read different paragraphs, and so forth.

Plan the Logistics of the Message

You'll need to choose a prominent spot for the message so that it greets students as they enter the room. Be sure to choose a spot that won't interrupt early morning traffic flow when several children are clustered together, reading or responding to the message. Keeping the message in the same spot every morning helps make it part of the classroom routine.

Many teachers like to use a chart stand and easel paper for their message. In most rooms, this makes the message easier to physically move and incorporate into the meeting circle. Using paper and markers also eliminates the risks of smudges and erasures and allows you to save the chart and post it after the meeting. Some teachers put old charts in the class library for students to read during language arts or send the charts home with individual children on a rotating basis.

Because of the cost of chart paper, some teachers prefer to use dry-erase boards. The boards work well in the moment but don't allow the teacher to save the message for later use. To address this, some teachers take digital pictures of the message each day and save the pictures for later use.

Still other teachers like to use an interactive whiteboard to write and post their message. They can save each day's message and print out a booklet of messages at the end of the year. If you're thinking about using this option, consider how to make the message part of the circle, which is helpful as students interact with the message during this fourth and final component of Morning Meeting. In one kindergarten classroom, the teacher organized her morning routine and meeting around the message location on the interactive whiteboard. Students hung their coats, moved their magnetic photos under the school lunch/home lunch columns (the teacher later completed attendance from this information), and then waited patiently to stand

---

Morning Message Topics

Here are some things to consider when deciding on the content of each day's message:

• **Is it current?** Focusing on current work or building on work from previous days sets the stage for the day ahead.

• **Is it inclusive?** Every message should speak to all class members. All students should see themselves mirrored in the message.

• **Is it engaging?** The most effective topics are those that interest all students. Varying topics from day to day and using examples drawn from classroom life can help keep student interest high.

Here's a starter list of possible message topics:

• A plant or animal the class is observing

• An activity the class will be doing that day, such as going to a special or on a field trip

• The class pet

• Current events

• Favorites (numbers, books, games, and so on)

• Healthy foods and other healthy habits

• Memories or predictions

• Riddles, puns, and wordplay

• Writing workshop topics or any content the class is studying

---

on the step stool to interact with the message before moving to the various morning activities in the room. When the teacher rang the chime, students gathered in the circle space located by the interactive whiteboard to participate in the Morning Meeting and engage with the message.

Regardless of the medium you choose, what matters most is that the message content is relevant to the current life of the classroom and that students can easily interact with the message. Consider any accessibility issues students in your class may face, such as visual impairments that might make handwriting difficult to read or sensory needs that mean students will benefit from being able to interact physically with the paper on which the message is written.

Tailor Content, Format, and Activities to Your Particular Class

Part of what makes a morning message of real interest to students is its pertinence to the classroom life of a particular group at a particular time. To be real and immediate, our messages must be specific to each day and class.

With younger groups in which most students are not yet fluent readers, even the predictable parts of the message are specific to the day, including such information as the date, the day's line leader, or a sentence about the weather. Additional content usually springs from current activities: "We will work with clay today," "Look at our egg before Morning Meeting," or "Draw a food you like."

When teaching older students with established reading skills, teachers have room for more variation in format, but the information should still derive from classroom activities and interests and should still be particular to the day. Perhaps it's World Series time and excitement is high; the message might feature a math problem involving statistics from yesterday's game. In another room, a teacher writes the question "Do you know what today is?" and then includes historical facts about the date, followed by open-ended questions. Down the hall, a different teacher uses a new vocabulary word every day in the message, being sure to choose a word relevant to what students will be working on that day. She uses the word in a sentence and then challenges students to figure out the meaning by using context clues.

Classroom community issues can also make good topics. Is a new student joining the class? You might prompt students to think about ways they can welcome them. Are students getting sloppy with cleanup after science experiments? Include a thinking question that helps them evaluate cleanup procedures. Were there problems during recess yesterday? The message might direct students to be prepared to share at Morning Meeting one way they can help make recess go more smoothly today.

Keep Messages Focused

Particularly in older grades, teachers are sometimes tempted to make the message comprehensive, squeezing in just one more thing students really ought to be thinking about, one more type of spelling error for them to find. This can get overwhelming, both for the students who read and act on the information and for the teacher who creates it.

Remember: the purposes of the morning message component are to welcome and greet students, to orient them and get them excited about their day, and to use the written format of the message for a quick warm-up skill-builder. Resist the temptation to launch into a spelling lesson based on an error students didn't catch or to list everything students will need to know about tomorrow's field trip.

Instead, file away the spelling error for a mini-lesson before writing time later in the week; then perhaps in the following week, feature some examples of words with that spelling pattern in the morning message. And if the field trip requires substantial reminders, a separate field trip meeting in the afternoon is in order.

Morning message, coming at the end of Morning Meeting, serves as a transition into the rest of the day. We want students to leave the meeting sensing their competence and feeling equipped to navigate their day. It's important, therefore, that these last few minutes of the meeting be well paced, calm, and uncluttered.

It's also helpful to keep the message visually, as well as informationally, clear and focused. Use just one easy-to-read color for most of the text and another, brighter color for highlighting a word or two or adding a simple decoration. Using many colors is cheerful but can also be overly stimulating.

Another way to keep the message focused is to avoid using the body of the message for announcements or reminders, such as "Put your writing journal in the basket on my table." Instead, set these aside in a bubble at the top or bottom of the message.

Finally, avoid posting the schedule for the day on the message—including the schedule each day can dilute the impact of the message. Although this information is important, write it in a separate place.

Decide Which Message Elements to Use

There are a number of elements commonly found in morning messages. Choose those that you think will be helpful for your class, such as some of these:

- **Greeting**—A salutation or heading opens the message. Many teachers use a letter salutation such as "Dear Second Graders" or "Good morning, Focused Workers!" No matter what the choice of words, the greeting is friendly in tone and tells students, "This message is written especially for you! Come and read it!"

- **Date**—You can date the message in various ways. For young children, using a consistent, predictable format is usually best. Teachers of emergent readers might begin with very simple structures, first writing "Today is [day of the week]" to teach the days of the week. They would then add statements about the month, date, and year, building to "Today is Monday, March 30, 2024." As children acquire calendar skills and learn the days of the week and the names of the months, some teachers leave parts of the date blank and have the group fill them in during Morning Meeting. In messages for more experienced readers, the date is usually located in a corner, as it would be in a letter. Students can benefit from seeing this information in a variety of formats: with and without abbreviations or in shorthand such as 3/30/24.

- **Body of the Message**—With the exception of very beginning readers and English speakers, students should be able to read and understand at least parts of the message before Morning Meeting, either independently or with assis-

Scan the QR code to see a teacher and class read the message in an interactive way.

tance from a classmate. Craft the reading level of your message with this in mind. In general, keep the language simple at the beginning of the year and increase the complexity as students are able to handle more sophisticated reading challenges. And throughout the year, continue to keep each message focused on one topic.

- **Related Interactive Tasks**—The message may conclude with a question to think about or a simple activity for students to complete before the meeting starts. Such interactive tasks are most effective when they go hand in hand with the body of the message, inviting students to interact in some way with what they've just read. For example, "Look for -*ing* words in this message and be ready to point to them" or "Find all of our word wall words in the message. Be ready to share them in our meeting." Keep in mind that the message is a place for quick warm-ups and skill practice. The tasks that work best are those that everyone in the group will be able to complete quickly, independently, and successfully.

- **Closing and Signature**—Many teachers who write messages in letter format use a closing that's in a respectful and professional voice,

Ways to Read Morning Messages as a Class

Choral read:
- Read in different voices (whisper, spooky, loud, soft).
- Take turns: divide group in half; one half reads a sentence (or paragraph) while the other listens; switch back and forth.

Echo read:
- The teacher or a student reads a sentence; rest of class echo reads same sentence.
- Have everyone read silently, then call on one student to paraphrase.

Pantomime read:
- Choose several words from the message, brainstorm ways to pantomime them, and then read the message together, inserting those actions at the appropriate spots.
- Chant or sing the message to a familiar tune.
- Add sound effects for punctuation marks.
- Say the salutation in another language, including American Sign Language.
- Clap the beats for words with two or more syllables.

such as "Sincerely," or "Your teacher," followed by their name or signature. Some teachers conclude with an encouraging phrase, such as "Let's have a great learning day!" or "Do your best!" The choice depends on what feels right for you and makes sense for a particular class.

Think About How the Class Will Work With the Message

Morning message gains its power from the interactions it generates—the teacher communicating with students and students communicating with one another as they read the message, independently and as a group, and complete any related tasks. For this reason, it's important to consider how you'll have students work with the message.

Before Morning Meeting

For most classes, the general expectation is that students will read the message and do any interactive tasks before Morning Meeting begins. Because students typically have several jobs to complete upon arrival in the classroom in the morning, it's important to explicitly teach the expectations for working with the message. Should students put away their backpacks and lunches, sign in, and then go over to read and interact with the message? Should they read and interact with the message before turning to their morning math challenge? Answer these questions clearly for yourself, and then teach the routine to the class.

When you introduce a new interactive task for students to do, such as using tally marks, filling in a Venn diagram, or putting data on a graph, be sure to model and practice it before asking students to do the task independently.

During Morning Meeting

In most classes, teachers begin the morning message component by leading the class in reading the message aloud. To keep things interesting, vary the way you read the message from day to day. Choral reading, line-by-line echo reading, and teacher or individual student reading can all work well. So can reading at different volumes or with different intonations. Keep in mind that students are generally more engaged with the message when they're reading it aloud, so limit the number of days when you have just one student read the message.

After reading the message, the class briefly discusses or works with the message in a way that expands on its content. For example, students might explore thinking questions posed in the message, comment on the message content, engage in skill practice embedded in the message, or make observations about what classmates wrote in the interactive portion of the message.

After Morning Meeting

Many teachers leave the message on display for the rest of the school day. This allows students to continue adding ideas. The message might also be used during lessons. A message that asks, "What do you know about salmon?" might be posted on a wall so that students can add answers for the duration of their salmon study. Over time, the document becomes a testament to the class's learning.

Sometimes, teachers will send message charts home with students on a rotating basis. One parent reported peeking into her son's room one evening to see that he had the day's message chart taped to his wall and was reading it aloud, using a ruler to point to each word. By sending message charts home, you can extend the power of Morning Meeting beyond the classroom walls.

Some teachers make a class book of the messages each month and keep the books in their class library for students to read. Others save messages for a year and then use them as part of year-end assessment projects. When the messages are spread out in a large space, they provide a powerful visual story of the year's learning.

Understand Morning Message Responsibilities

In implementing and assessing morning message, keep the following general responsibilities in mind.

Teacher's responsibilities:

- Prepare the message before students arrive.

- Model neat handwriting and correct grammar and punctuation in the written message (unless you're deliberately embedding errors for students to correct).

- Incorporate current curriculum into the message and any related interactive tasks.

- Vary the kinds of skills required in related interactive tasks.

- Select an appropriate format for reading the message during the meeting and vary the format regularly.

- Choose individual students to unscramble, decode, find errors, and so on, while still keeping the whole group involved.

Students' responsibilities:

- Read the message upon entering the room.

- Follow any directions in the message.

- Read or follow along with the reading of the message during Morning Meeting.

- Participate in discussion or work based on the message before or during Morning Meeting.

Common Questions

Q **Students really like reading the morning message, but I find it hard to keep thinking of new things to write each day. I feel like it's taking me more time than it should to prepare the message. How can I come up with new ideas?**

A You have lots of company, particularly among teachers in the upper elementary grades. The predictable sentence starters and additional sentence or two that are just right for younger students are not challenging enough for older students.

Remember the recommendation from the Getting Started section about using the daily life of the classroom as a springboard for your message. Look to your ongoing curriculum and to your general observations and knowledge of your class for ideas rather than trying to think of fascinating, original tidbits. Do your students adore jokes and riddles? Are codes really fun for them right now? Are they all excited about the upcoming basketball season?

Some teachers have found that having a different but predictable topic for each day of the week helps them vary the content of their messages while removing the stress of total invention. Monday's message might always feature a question or tally about weekend activities, Tuesday's message might pose a math problem, Wednesday's might have a literacy focus, and Thursday's a topic from the social curriculum, such as how to take care of a guest teacher. To end the week, you could choose something from another content area or a current event.

There are also a number of books with ideas for morning message and all other Morning Meeting components, such as the *80 Morning Meeting Ideas* books and the Doing Academics In Morning Meeting series, all of which are available at www.responsiveclassroom.org.

Q **I have a class of twenty-seven fifth graders. We often don't have time for more than a quick reading of the message, particularly if our group activity has really grabbed the students. What can I do?**

A It's fine to vary the time spent on each meeting component based on your judgments about your class and what works for them—just be careful that the same component, such as morning message, doesn't always get cut short.

Some decisions about time variations happen on the spot. Perhaps a particularly riveting sharing prompts a deeper-than-usual exchange of questions, answers, and comments, and the teacher judges that it's worth cutting into group activity and message time to allow this fruitful conversation.

Other times, teachers know in advance that they'll need extra time for a particular meeting component and plan to shorten other components. Perhaps group activity needs to go a bit longer than usual because the teacher wants to introduce a new word game. Or perhaps the sharing component needs more time for students to share the models of solar-powered appliances they've been building in science. In such cases, an awareness of pacing will allow enough time for the group to fully engage in each component while not letting things drag or causing the meeting to extend beyond thirty minutes. However, while being flexible, teachers should keep in mind the purposes and elements of each component of Morning Meeting and make sure that all are encompassed over time—but not necessarily in each meeting.

Q **Are there special considerations I should keep in mind when I write the messages to ensure they are inclusive?**

A Morning message is a wonderful tool for developing language skills with students. Some students with limited English or language proficiency may need extra support to ensure the message is a source of joy rather than frustration. Here are some ideas and caveats:

- Enlist the help of support staff. For example, you could give the message to a paraprofessional to review with the student(s) before the meeting.

- Have the student work with a buddy who reads the message with them during arrival and uses gestures or other visuals to support understanding.

- To build vocabulary, spend some time before reading the message to preteach tricky words to students as a whole group. You might also develop a method where students put a check beside a word in the message to indicate that they need an explanation.

- Use print rather than cursive when writing the message. Reading cursive can be challenging for students with dyslexia or individuals just beginning to read English.

- Add visual cues, such as pictures or sketches, to help students understand new words.

- When writing more complex messages, create a simplified version with visuals for a student to read before the meeting. You might even store these simplified messages in a folder for the student to reference later.

- Be wary of embedding deliberate mistakes for students to correct in the message. Students with dyslexia or autism, as well as students with limited English proficiency, may be confused, thinking the mistakes are actually correct renderings.

Q It's the middle of the year, and very few of my students are reading and interacting with the message before the meeting. What should I do to increase participation?

A The first thing to do is to step back and review your messages and plans for working with them. Do they reflect classroom life? Are the interactive tasks varied? Have you included content that will engage students?

One teacher reports that when she first began doing Morning Meeting, she also noticed a midyear lull in morning message participation and decided to ask the students about it. She told them that she'd noticed that only a few of them were reading and responding to the message each day. Why might that be? The honest and articulate nine- and ten-year-olds responded very kindly but matter-of-factly: "Well, to be honest, they're not so interesting to read—they basically say the same thing every day. We know we have music on Thursdays and art on Fridays."

Aha! She realized she had started using the messages mostly for announcements and reminders. She wasn't putting enough thought into making them interesting and engaging for students, just as a good book would be. If she wanted students to read the message, she needed to vary what she did each day and put something in each message that would capture their attention.

As she probed a bit more, she discovered that some students had difficulty reading the message independently. So, along with making them more engaging, she needed to simplify the language to be sure that they appealed to readers at a variety of levels.

Finally, she noticed that some students struggled with organizational skills and just plain forgot to read the message or ran out of time for it because they got caught up in other morning tasks.

To address the issue of varied reading levels and to help students with organization, the teacher started using "message partners." She carefully considered students' strengths and challenges in reading, focus, and organizational skills and paired them up accordingly so that a student strong in one area, such as reading, was paired with someone who might struggle with reading. Or she would pair a student who had competent organizational skills with a student who had trouble getting tasks done. Each morning, the partners would get together and read and interact with the message.

Q **Students arrive at different times at my school. How do I make sure all have a chance to work with the message before Morning Meeting?**

A One way to deal with this issue is to prioritize morning tasks, emphasizing that reading and interacting with the message should be the first task accomplished.

Another idea is to have early arrivers assist late arrivers in working with the message. You can pair early and late arrivers: this can be one consideration as you assign "message partners" (see the preceding question). To save time, the early arriver can summarize the message and explain the related interactive task (if you've included one) or help with tasks such as turning in homework or hanging up a backpack. This gives the late arriver more time to read and interact with the message.

Many teachers also choose to leave the morning message up after Morning Meeting is over. This allows late arrivals to interact with the message whenever they arrive or during a specific time, such as snack. It also serves as a reference for all students to help them remember important information from the message, such as what skills they'll be focusing on that day or any special events or reminders for the day.

Morning Message Ideas

Kindergarten Messages

Good Morning!

Today is Tuesday.

It is sunny.

We will plant seeds.

Fondly,
Miss Cutter

Ideas for working with the message:

- Have students find and underline word wall words that are in the message.

- Echo read the message.

- Help children look ahead to their day with questions like these:

   ○ What kinds of seeds do you know about or have you seen before?

   ○ What kinds of seeds do you think we might plant in our classroom this afternoon?

Dear Kindergartners,

Today is Monday.

It is cold and windy outside.

In our book today, do you think Junie B. Jones will find her gloves?

Yes	No
✓✓✓ ✓✓	✓ ✓✓

Ideas for working with the message:

- Read the message to the class and then have the whole class read it chorally.

- Ask a few questions about students' predictions:

  ○ What do you think happened to Junie B. Jones's gloves?

  ○ Where do you think she might find them?

  ○ What do you think she will do when she finds them?

  ○ Why are those gloves so important to her?

Good Morning!

Today is Tuesday, October 21st.

We will think about soil.

Look at the soil in the plants in our room. Be ready to share something you notice or know about soil.

Love,
Mrs. Bonds

Ideas for working with the message:
- Chorally read the message.

- Invite a few students to share their thoughts.

Today is Thursday, April 17th.

Anna is first today.

We will have time to play
our song in music today!

What is your favorite
song? What is your favorite
instrument? Be ready to share.

Ideas for working with the message:

- Chorally read and add in sound effects for each type of punctuation.

- Ask children to name the punctuation signs they see in the message.

- Invite children to make the sound of the instrument they've named.

October 5, 2022

Dear Math Experts,

How many buttons do we all have today? We'll look at our graph during math later this morning.

Count the buttons on your clothing. Then put a sticker on our line graph to show how many buttons you have:

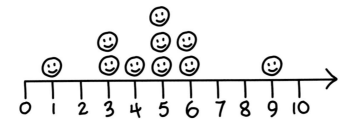

Ideas for working with the message:

- Echo read the message, line by line.

- Reflect on the data students provided. Here are some questions you could ask:

    ○ What is the greatest number of buttons someone has?

    ○ What is the least?

    ○ What number do you think is in the middle?

    ○ What are some ways we could add up all the buttons we have?

Thursday, May 11, 2023

Dear Geologists:

You have learned a lot about how wind and water can change the shape of land. Can you think of ways we could prevent wind and water from reshaping the land? Hmm. Talk about your ideas with a partner.

Write one idea below (if someone already wrote your idea put a check mark by it):

tall fence ✓
thick bushes

Ideas for working with the message:

- Brainstorm ways students can use their bodies to show wind or water.

- Chorally read the message. Whenever you get to the word *wind* or *water*, students can show their ideas from the brainstorming.

- Read the ideas that students wrote, ask a few students to explain their thinking, and add any new ideas.

Tuesday, Nov. 8, 2022

Dear Friendly Workers,

We have been practicing giving compliments to each other. Today in Writers' Workshop, we will be doing peer conferences. What might be something that you could compliment your writing partner about? Write your idea below.

Your teacher,
Mrs. Davis

Ideas for working with the message:

- Chorally read the message.

- Have a brief discussion about compliments. Possible questions:

  - Why do we give compliments?

  - What are some things to remember when giving a compliment to someone?

  - How does it feel to receive a compliment?

  - What might you do when you receive a compliment?

4/1/2022

Hello, Tricksters, and Happy April Fools' Day!

Some historians believe that April Fools' Day began in France in 1582. Before that time, New Year's Day was April 1st. Then France began using a different calendar, and New Year's Day was on January 1st. Those who continued to celebrate the new year in April were called "April Fools."

Have you ever played a trick on someone on April Fools' Day? Place a tally mark below:

Yes	No

I will definitely be on my toes today!
Mrs. Roser

Ideas for working with the message:

- Divide the group in two and alternate reading the message sentence by sentence.

- Ask questions to facilitate discussion:

   - Where can we go to find out facts about holidays?

   - When is trick-playing fun for everyone? When might it hurt someone's feelings? How could we take care of each other?

   - Why might it be important to be able to laugh at ourselves sometimes?

Fourth Grade Messages

Monday, January 16, 2023

Good Morning, Space Explorers!

Did you know that gravity is stronger on Earth than it is on the moon? In fact, things weigh only 1/6 as much on the moon. What would you be able to do if you weighed so much less? What wouldn't you be able to do? Be ready to share during our meeting.

Ideas for working with the message:

- Have students silently read the message, then ask for a student to paraphrase it.

- Help students understand 1/6, if needed.

- Ask volunteers to share answers to the questions and their reasoning.

2/10/23

Dear Awesome Artists,

Your illustrations for our class read-aloud books are fantastic! They show such a rich variety of ideas and feelings about the book. I would like to display all of your illustrations for everyone to see. Let's brainstorm some interesting ways that we might arrange this display. Be ready to share your ideas.

Have a great learning day!

Mrs. Hofmann

Ideas for working with the message:

- Divide the class into two groups and alternate reading the message sentence by sentence.

- Have students talk with partners about ways to create a display, then invite volunteers to share their ideas with the whole group.

- Ask for students' ideas about whether illustrations should be grouped by style, topic, or some other organizing principle.

September 28, 2022

Dear Friends of the Outdoors,

Before we start our new unit on nature, I am wondering . . . What is one thing you love about the great outdoors? Write it in a box below with your name.

WHAT I LOVE ABOUT NATURE:

QUOTE OF THE DAY:

"To me a lush carpet of pine needles or spongy grass is more welcome than the most luxurious Persian rug."
—Helen Keller

Ideas for working with the message:

- Go around the circle, having each person read one word of the message.

- Have a few students read their response aloud and invite anyone who has a connection to it to give a "Me, too" signal.

- Lead a brief discussion about the quote and what students are most looking forward to learning about nature.

March 31, 2023

Dear **Amiable** Students,

I love reading so much that sometimes I worry that I read **excessively**! Do you think it's possible to read too much? Do you ever worry that you spend too much time doing just one thing?

Managing time well is a valuable skill. So, let's think about how we can **evaluate** our use of time. Write one idea below.

Your **affable** teacher,
Mrs. Kimbell

Ideas for working with the message:

- Discuss the meaning and pronunciation of the bolded words. You might ask, "Can you figure out the meaning of the words using context clues?"

- Brainstorm with students a quick gesture to use for each of the bold words, then read the message together, doing the motion for each bold word.

- Invite a few students to share their ideas for how to evaluate their use of time and how to use time more wisely.

Special Message: Birthday

On students' birthdays, write a birthday morning message that includes some specific things the class knows about that student. Students can interact with the message by wishing their classmate a happy birthday or just adding their name.

Good Morning!

Today is Natalie's birthday! Natalie, we are so happy to have you in our class! We hope you get to celebrate by eating glazed donuts and playing basketball with your friends.

Leave a message or sign your name below
to wish Natalie a happy birthday!

Ideas for working with the message:

- Instead of making the whole message for the individual student, include "Happy birthday, ___!" at the end of the Morning Message. Allow students to interact with the message by adding a special note or birthday wish to the bottom of the message. At the end of the morning, cut the bottom of the message off and send it home with the birthday student.

- Write the message in the birthday student's favorite color. You could even include a photo of them on the message.

- If the student's birthday falls on the weekend, make this message either the Friday before or the Monday after.

- For younger students, draw a bunch of balloons and have students write their name in the balloons.

Special Message: Holiday

Create a brief message including language, pictures, symbols, and a little history about the holiday. Print small color photos of people celebrating this holiday, symbols, and traditions to place around the message. You can also use these for a share or activity, as well. These pictures will add engagement and excitement about the holiday you are sharing about, whether it is familiar to your students or not.

Eid Mubarak!

Eid al-Fitr, also known as just Eid, is a Muslim holiday that marks the end of Ramadan, the Islamic month of fasting. Celebrations could include gathering together with friends and family, decorating homes, eating special sweet foods, and exchanging presents.

Does your family celebrate Eid al-Fitr? Do you know someone who does? Would you like to know more? Write your initials in the stars below. We'll talk more about this during Morning Meeting.

We celebrate!

I know someone who does!

I want to know more!

Ideas for working with the message:

- Create a list of holidays based on what your communities celebrate so that you are ready to write holiday messages. Ask your students and their families for ideas!

- To adapt for use on interactive boards, use clip art or insert photos instead of printing. Consider using an interactive feature to have students move their names or write on the board.

Harnessing the Power of Morning Meeting

The gymnasium is full to bursting, with five hundred students and staff sitting in folding chairs or cross-legged on the floor. Usually, this space is used for physical education classes, for recess when it is raining, and sometimes for rehearsals before a big performance. But once a month, the space is transformed into an all-school gathering space for the community to come together in a schoolwide Morning Meeting. Everyone comes: each student and teacher has a spot, every member of the support staff is present, and some parents and family members have come to participate. Even front office staff members have left their desks and come to the gym to be part of this joyful gathering.

The sound of five hundred voices calling to each other, sneakers squeaking against the polished floor, and the door opening and closing fill the room. There is so much to see in that space that most of the students haven't noticed that their principal, Mrs. Young, has moved to the front of the room. She looks out at the sea of excited faces and smiles. One or two teachers meet her eyes; some of the older students in the back of the room sit up a little straighter in their seats. Everyone else keeps on chatting, laughing, and enjoying each other's company.

Mrs. Young holds a chime in one hand and a small mallet in the other. As she carefully taps the mallet just once on the metal rod of the chime, a powerful tone resonates around the room. At first, it is loud enough to be heard just for a moment above the sea of voices, many of which pause mid-sentence as soon as the chime sounds. As the tone reverberates throughout the room, it gets quieter and quieter. However, it can still be heard clearly because, one by one, the voices stop. The sneakers hold still. And the door is finally closed. All eyes are on Mrs. Young. After a few seconds, the entire room is completely silent, save for the final echo of the chime.

Something special is about to begin.

What Is a Schoolwide Morning Meeting?

A schoolwide Morning Meeting is a school assembly that follows the four-part structure of a classroom Morning Meeting. Some schools choose to call this assembly by another name such as town hall, community connection, or a school-specific name. Regardless of what it's called, the schoolwide Morning Meeting serves specific purposes within the overall school community.

Purposes and Goals of Schoolwide Morning Meeting

In the classroom, Morning Meeting connects students as a community of learners poised to experience their best selves in the day of learning ahead. At the schoolwide level, the purposes are to help students understand they are part of something bigger than their own class experience and to realize that, while they are busy in their own classrooms, they are working alongside other learners throughout the school.

A well-crafted schoolwide Morning Meeting:

- Builds affiliation and pride among students and between students and teachers

- Creates and celebrates schoolwide rituals and shared experiences

- Provides an opportunity to develop and practice social, emotional, and academic competencies within a large-group setting

Building Affiliation and Community

School affiliation and pride is the idea of feeling connected to the school community and joyful about being part of it. This sense of belonging and pride has positive impacts on students individually and collectively. For students, positive engagement with peers and teachers has been shown to impact academic performance. One research project by Varsity Brands illustrated that students with higher levels of school pride are more likely to perform better academically, are more civically engaged, and are also happier (Varsity Brands 2014). Schoolwide Morning Meetings, which celebrate class groups in a joyful manner, are powerful instruments to help build affiliation and pride by creating memorable, shared experiences that celebrate the community. Schoolwide Morning Meetings model the positive culture of the school.

Celebrating Rituals and Shared Experiences

Rituals and shared experiences are the glue that bring a school culture together. They are powerful ways to both create and communicate school culture. The four-part Morning Meeting structure in itself is a powerful ritual as it provides familiarity, predictability, and flexibility. Within this structure, there are opportunities for students to share songs, dances, performances, and ideas that both highlight their unique contributions to the overall school community and invite the community to share these experiences.

For example, as older students share a presentation about a classroom project with the school community, they are able to highlight their accomplishments and give children in the younger grades something to look forward to in the coming years. And as younger students share their learning with the community, they practice the skills they saw modeled by the older students, who can remember fondly their own time in that grade. When older and younger students can share experiences and memories like that, it creates a powerful bond and sense of community. Older students can be role models, and younger students have someone to look up to. Importantly, older students can also see tangible proof of their own growth and development when they see their younger schoolmates share and remember being in their shoes. At the same time, younger students develop a sense of hope and enthusiasm for the future when they see, in their older schoolmates' presentations, what lies ahead for them.

Developing Social, Emotional, and Academic Competencies

As students gather in the larger group, they might work collectively with their class to guess the answer to a riddle, exhibit self-control amid a vast amount of stimuli, and give attention to someone sharing from far away. By doing so, the schoolwide meeting provides students with a unique opportunity to develop and practice skills needed to navigate a large-group setting. It's also an opportunity to hone social and emotional learning skills such as cooperation, assertiveness, responsibility, empathy, and self-control. The development of these skills can greatly impact interactions in the hallways, lunchrooms, playgrounds, and buses as students navigate how to be one among hundreds versus one among twenty. Developing these skills also contributes to the academic life of children, helping them to be mindful participants in the classroom.

Getting Started

The notion of bringing together the entire school community and leading them through a schoolwide Morning Meeting may seem daunting. Standing in front of hundreds of students and colleagues can be intimidating. Will the crowd be able to settle down and listen? Will children and adults want to participate? Will the time feel engaging and meaningful? The answer to all of those questions is a resounding yes—with planning, practice, and time!

There are several strategies that lead to successful schoolwide Morning Meetings, and they will be familiar ones for educators who have implemented classroom Morning Meetings. Teaching meeting-related routines in advance, using visual and auditory signals, and planning carefully are crucial. It's also important to start small and work up to more involved meetings. Laying a strong foundation with these strategies will help make the experience for participants and leaders alike feel more comfortable until, eventually, it becomes second nature.

Laying the Foundation

Bringing together the entire school community is not a small feat! It's crucial to gather a team within your school to plan and implement schoolwide meetings to ensure that they run as safely and smoothly as possible. Here are some points to consider:

Space—Examine the proposed space to make sure it is adequate to support a schoolwide Morning Meeting. Look at the flow and consider limitations. For example, if the only space available has auditorium-style seating, it will change the approach to certain components.

Seating—When evaluating the space, also consider how adults might be able to supervise and support students when they are seated. While it might seem logical to have an entire class in one long row, consider how the teacher will be able to redirect a student on the opposite end of the row if the need arises. For this reason, it might help to seat students in clusters. This allows the teacher to maintain proximity and be close to more students throughout the experience. Mark each area with a marker, such as a cone or sign, to help all gather into the space easily.

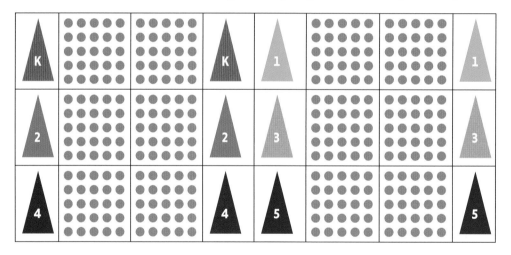

Sound and Sight—Check the auditory and visual setup of the space. Attention can quickly wane when there are audio and visual distractions and distortions. Ensure that everyone can see the message and clearly hear the speaker. Determine if microphones and a sound system need to be used, and arrange for support with those systems during the meeting.

Signal for Attention—After determining how to physically bring the entire community into one space, getting everyone's attention will be the first important task to master. Auditory and/or visual signals for attention are an important way to mark the beginning of the meeting, get participants' attention, and refocus the group as needed.

Auditory Signals

When establishing an auditory signal, choose one that can be heard by all. A handheld chime rung in proximity to a microphone works well. Auditory signals should be used at the start of the meeting when bringing the group together. The sound can also be helpful to refocus students when they are participating in aspects of the meeting that require conversation or movement.

Visual Signals

Visual signals are also important to have, especially ones that can be quickly replicated by other adults and students and help facilitate gathering students back together. Simple ideas include a raised hand or a raised hand accompanied by a single finger over the lips to signal quiet.

Depending on the group size, it can be helpful to use a signal that is both auditory and visual. Ringing a handheld chime works well as it creates a sound to begin the process of gathering everyone back together while also providing a visual reminder that sustains students until everyone has turned their attention to the meeting leader.

Routines and Procedures—When examining the space and considering the logistical flow of the meeting, think about aspects of the routine to be named and modeled. Classroom teachers will be instrumental in teaching many of these routines, although it will be critical that the entire staff understands what these will look, sound, and feel like in action. Here are a few routines that will need to be established and taught to students:

- Entering and exiting the assembly space
- Responding to the signal for attention
- Turning and talking with a partner
- Speaking into a microphone
- Standing and then sitting back in the same spot

Before bringing students into the space for the first schoolwide meeting, give them a preview of what to expect. Prior to assembling as a group, classroom teachers should teach and model some of the routines and procedures. Individual classes should practice going into the space, finding their seats, and practicing what will be expected of them prior to the first schoolwide meeting.

Meeting Rules—The school community's rules should be established and visually present in the meeting space. As part of the opening of the meeting, students should take some time to connect with the school rules. Teachers will play a large part in helping students to consider how the rules might apply to the assembly setting. It is also important to refer to these rules as a helpful reminder of the expectations throughout the assembly. For instance, the meeting leader could say, "As we settle in today, take one minute to think about how these rules might help our meeting be safe, joyful, and engaging," or "As we begin by doing our greeting, take a moment to think about what rule you want to keep in mind during this meeting."

Scaffolding for Success

As with classroom Morning Meetings, it's important to start schoolwide Morning Meetings with low-risk, straightforward components and slowly increase complexity over time. Establishing a strong foundation first allows the community to safely and successfully build up to more complicated activities over the course of the school year. Here are two considerations to keep in mind:

- **Start Small**—When introducing the schoolwide Morning Meeting, it can be helpful to start with only one or two components, such as a greeting and a message. This will allow the entire student body to practice getting into the space together and requires minimal stamina in the first weeks of the school year in order to sustain a positive experience. When the community is ready, move on to a simple leader-led meeting that incorporates all four components but requires minimal movement.

- **Slowly Increase Complexity**—Start by having a consistent leader, such as the school principal, for the meeting. As the school community becomes more accustomed to participating in schoolwide meetings, include other meeting leaders to keep the meeting time new and exciting. This might mean involving other school or district staff, asking a classroom or special subject teacher to lead a meeting, or even having grade levels or classes host meetings.

Schoolwide Morning Meeting In Action

Because schoolwide Morning Meetings build upon the familiar structure of classroom Morning Meetings, many of the ideas within this book can be quickly adapted for use in a schoolwide setting. When adapting an idea for a large group, consider how to adjust to the group's size and meet the goals of the school community. Here are a few considerations and ideas to try out.

Greeting

Being seen and recognized by name as part of the larger school community is important. How that happens with hundreds of students will look different than it does within a classroom. In a large-group meeting, a class is acknowledged as a group, rather than as individuals. Also, it is wise, at first, to use greetings that require minimal movement. Eventually, more complex greetings where students exit their seated area and move throughout the space are possible in communities that have a lot of experience with schoolwide meetings.

Here are some greetings to try out.

Different Languages for Greeting (adapted)

The meeting leader can greet each class in a language other than English. The use of different languages for greeting can be incorporated into many greeting structures. Some options include:

- American Sign Language (signing "hello" is similar to saluting: with the fingers squeezed together and the palm facing outward, touch the tips of the fingers to the forehead and then move the hand slightly forward and then sharply down)

- Marhaba (Arabic)
- Bonjou (Haitian Creole)
- Bonjour (French)
- Buenos días (Spanish)
- Buon giorno (Italian)
- Dobroe utro (Russian)
- Guten morgen (German)
- Jambo (Swahili)
- Dzień dobry (Polish)
- Kalimera (Greek)
- Namaste (Hindi)
- Ni hao (Mandarin Chinese)
- Ohay (Japanese)
- Shalom (Hebrew)
- Xin chào (Vietnamese)

For example:

Principal Smith:	"Bonjour, Ms. Apple's class."
Ms. Apple's class, in unison:	"Bonjour, Principal Smith!"

One, Two, Three, Four (adapted)

Prior to the meeting, tell classes they need to come up with a movement to share with the entire school. Use the chant below for the greeting. This can be chanted or sung. When a class or grade level is called, they stand and do whatever movement they want as a class—for example, a bow, curtsy, wave, dance, or wiggle—while the rest of the students sing or chant. As the school sings/chants the last line, the grade level/class sits back down. Another class is called and the process is repeated.

Chant:
One, two, three, four.
Come on [grade level/class], hit the floor.
We're so glad you're here today.
Hurray, hurray, hurray!

Cheer (adapted)

Have students name an activity they like to do as a class prior to coming to the meeting. Going around the room, classes do the following call-and-response greeting:

Class:	We are [class name].
School:	YEAH!
Class:	And we like to [activity].
School:	Uh-huh.
Class:	And we'll be a [class who does this activity].
School:	YEAH!
Class:	Every day of our life.
Group:	Every day of their life.

Sharing

The sharing component requires students to be able to pay attention and listen to the speaker in order to make and build connections. In larger spaces, this can prove challenging for many students. To make sharing work well in a large-group setting, we recommend three strategies that work well as students build their stamina with speaking and listening activities in a crowd:

- Take volunteers to share with the group using a microphone.

- Do a partner sharing where students turn and talk with someone in close proximity.

- Use nonverbal signals to make connections.

Here are some sharing ideas to try.

Fill in the Blank (adapted)

Have classes share a response to a fill-in-the-blank sentence. The students in the class can shout responses to their teacher. The teacher will pick a response for the class and share.

For example: Our favorite lunch menu item is _____.

Headline News (adapted)

In advance, give each class index cards and invite them to write a headline about themselves (for example, "This Weekend Brings a Surprise Visitor," "*Bud, Not Buddy* Is Our Favorite Book," "Field Trip Planned Next Week"). As they enter, the teacher should give the card to the leader.

The leader reads each card and takes a few guesses from the audience about which class it might be. If they don't guess correctly after a couple of tries, the headline classroom stands and says, "That's us!"

Dialogue Sharing (adapted)

The speaker shares the topic ahead of time with teachers and students. In the classroom, the teacher helps students think of questions or comments. Each classroom brings a question or comment to the schoolwide meeting. As the speaker shares, they ask for questions or comments and respond to three or four questions posed by classes.

Activity

Activities are great unifiers that build a repertoire of well-loved songs, games, chants, and other shared experiences. It is also often the most highly energized portion of a Morning Meeting and can quickly go awry within a large-group setting. For this reason, it can help to use activities that require minimal movement or movement that can be done in unison.

Here are some activities to try.

Laughing Handkerchief

Throw up a cloth handkerchief or towel. Tell students they can laugh as hard as they can until the handkerchief hits the ground.

Variation: Hold up the handkerchief in the air and tell students they can laugh until the handkerchief comes down and goes behind your back. Then hold it up and bring it down, placing it behind your back at various rates.

Aroostasha (adapted)

Students stand with their hands clasped in front of them, fingers interlaced. Begin the activity by demonstrating the chant and body movements. Chant "Aroostasha, aroostasha, aroostasha-sha" while moving your clasped hands from the right side of your body to the left and pulsing your hands up and down to the beat. Then do the chant while moving your hands back to the right side of your body, pulsing to the beat as you go. Have the class repeat the chant and body movements after you.

Call out "thumbs up"; then chant and do the above movement with hands clasped and thumbs up. Call out "thumbs up, wrists together," and do the chant and movement with hands clasped, thumbs up, and wrists together.

Keep going in this way, adding one body position at a time. For example, you can add:

- Elbows in

- Knees together

- Toes in

- Bottom out

- Tongue out (Ever try to say "Aroostasha" with your tongue out? Kids really get a laugh out of this!)

Human Protractor Variation

Everyone stands touching toes. Tell students they're going to straighten up gradually, keeping their arms stretched out in front of their bodies. At the same time, they'll be counting from zero to five. By the time their hands are reaching overhead, they should be at the upper number. Let students know that they need to remember where their hands are at different numbers. Then have them rate different activities on a scale from zero to five, with zero being least favorite and five being their absolute favorite. Call out an activity and have them show you where they would rate that activity.

Message

The message can serve as a road map for what students can expect in the meeting and be a powerful way to build excitement about what lies ahead. When crafting the message, be certain to create one that is large enough for all to see. If the meeting space has a projector, it's helpful to project the message on a large screen. It can also help to distribute copies of the messages to teachers on large pieces of paper so that they can reinforce and support reading the message.

Providing a thinking prompt in the message is a useful way to both make the message interactive and give students something to discuss. As classes arrive, students can participate in a partner chat or small-group chat until the meeting begins. When the message is explored at the end of the meeting, a few teachers or students can share some responses.

Here are some message ideas to try.

Message in Motion (adapted)

Choose words in the message and then choose volunteers to make up a motion for words in the message. Have the entire student body practice making the chosen motions to the chosen words. Then read the message using the motions as those words are read.

Voice Reading (adapted)

Pick a voice to read the message in (loud, soft, whisper, excited, etc.). Have the entire student body read the message in that voice.

Sample Schoolwide Meeting Plans

Every group and every space are unique, so planning a schoolwide morning meeting will be a process specific to your school setting. Determining the right combination of greeting, sharing, group activity, and morning message may be your first step. Considering the logistics of adapting those ideas to a larger group will be a close second.

What follows are two versions of what a schoolwide Morning Meeting plan might look like, first for a meeting led by an individual leader and then for a meeting led by a class or group. While your meetings may not look exactly like these, the plans can be models for how to adapt activities and plan out a successful schoolwide meeting.

Leader-Led Meeting

Adjective Greeting Variation
The leader uses adjectives to describe a group as they greet that group. Example:
Leader: Good morning, kind kindergarten.
Kindergarten class: Good morning, Mr. Vega.

Fill in the Blank
Each class shares a response to the sentence "Our favorite thing to do at recess is_____."

Take Sides
Make up a list of contrasting statements about students' preferences. For example, "I love to sleep late" and "I love to get up early," or "I like to be with big groups" and "I like to be with one friend." Draw an imaginary line down the middle of the space and designate opposing sides of the room. Then call out a pair of statements. Students for whom the first statement is true point to the left; students for whom the second statement is true point to the right. Students who don't feel strongly about either statement keep hands down.

Message in Motion
Choose words in the message and then choose volunteers to make up a motion for words in the message. Have the entire student body practice making the chosen motions to the chosen words. Then read the message using the motions as those words are read.

Class-Led Meeting

Greeting

One, Two, Three, Four
For this greeting, the entire school chants or sings the greeting below while each class shares a movement. Prior to the meeting, tell classes they need to come up with a movement to share with the entire school. When a grade level/class is called, they stand and do whatever movement they want as a class (for example, a bow, curtsy, wave, dance, or wiggle) while the rest of the students sing or chant. As the school sings/chants the last line, the grade level/class sits back down. Another class's name is called and the process is repeated.
> Chant:
> One, two, three, four
> Come on [grade level/class], hit the floor.
> We're so glad you're here today.
> Hurray, hurray, hurray!

Sharing

Dialogue Sharing
A chosen student representative shares a grade-level/class learning experience. They then take questions from a few members of the audience.

Activity

Cooper Says
Activity is like Simon Says, but no one is ever out. The leader, "Cooper," gives the group instructions. Everyone follows the instructions only if preceded by "Cooper says . . ." Keep the activity moving quickly.

Message

Voice Reading
The class/grade level picks a voice style for the entire student body to use while reading the message.

Investing in Morning Meeting

Seeing the entire school community experiencing joy together can be a powerful thing. The schoolwide meeting provides a profound glimpse into the culture of the school. It tells a story of school identity, shared values, and important commonalities. This powerful gathering can be shared with other school constituents, including parents and other community members. Welcoming more people to schoolwide meetings has the potential to cultivate a more unified sense of community and school pride.

Invite parents and community members. The best way to establish or influence the perception of a school is to provide an experience that evokes emotion and joy. Parents and communities want the best for their schools and the students they serve. By inviting parents and community members to your schoolwide meetings, you help them gain a better sense of your school. For this reason, it can be helpful to hold schoolwide meetings at predictable times that might make it convenient for parents and community members to attend, such as at the end of the day on the third Thursday of each month. These events can also appear on the school calendar along with other major events. You can also leverage technology for those parents and community members who can't attend in person, by obtaining appropriate permissions and live streaming events on secured, invitation-only portals.

Do more than meet. Providing a participatory role for parents in the schoolwide meeting is a surefire way to cultivate their wholehearted engagement. Having a special greeting with movement for parents is one way of doing this. Encouraging their participation in sharing, or even giving a parent a leadership role in facilitating an activity, could be other ways.

While parents or community members are in the building to witness their child experiencing the joy of the meeting, make a point to give them additional glimpses at the great work the school is doing. Place student artwork or academic projects on display as a reminder of what the community can accomplish. Frame or mount the work with the same reverence as an art piece in the large-group gathering areas. Consider holding informal meetings following the schoolwide meeting, or simply provide a reception for parents and community members to build connections. Do be cautious in scheduling too many agenda-driven meetings in conjunction with the invitation to a schoolwide meeting. One of the best ways to get parents invested is just to let them feel a part of something without obligation.

Not all parents will be able to attend schoolwide Morning Meetings, but you can still ensure that the entire community feels connected to those gatherings. Post photos from each meeting on your school's website or social media accounts, share updates in newsletters, and talk about this important tradition at open houses, back-to-school nights, and other events.

Adult Morning Meetings

Morning Meeting can also be a positive influence on other constituencies within your school, such as a staff community or parent group. Using the familiar four-part structure of Morning Meeting contributes to a sense of unity, creates community within the adult group, and provides a familiar scaffolding. Here are some other ways the Morning Meeting structure can be used:

Staff Meeting—The Morning Meeting format can be used at staff meetings to both strengthen adult community and address topics at hand.

Example Staff Meeting—Addressing Issues on the Playground

Ball Toss
Someone begins by greeting another person and then gently throwing, rolling, or bouncing a ball to them. The second person returns the greeting (but not the ball). They then choose a new colleague to greet and pass the ball to. Continue in this way until all have been greeted once. The greeting ends when the ball returns to the starter. If you're using a small, soft ball, throwing underhand works best. Roll or softly bounce a large, bouncy ball.

Partner Sharing
What is one thing you notice about our recess space and what is one wish?

A Warm Wind Blows
Bring chairs into the meeting circle—the number of chairs should be one less than the number of people in the circle. Everyone sits except for one person who stands in the middle of the circle. That person says, "A warm wind blows for anyone who _____," filling in the blank with a category (for example, "has a dog"). Everyone who fits that category comes into the center of the circle and then quickly finds a new place to sit, including the person who started in the middle. The one person who doesn't find a seat now stands in the center of the circle and says, "A warm wind blows for anyone who _____," naming a new category. The activity continues for several rounds. Encourage individuals to name categories that relate to interests, hobbies, and family rather than clothing or appearance. You could brainstorm a list of categories before beginning the activity.

Message and Reflection
The topic for this staff meeting is recess. Post a message about recess at the beginning of the meeting, and as teachers enter ask them to respond to the prompt about recess in the message.

> Dear Staff,
> Recess is an important part of the day. It provides an opportunity for students to connect and experience important free play. It can also be a time of conflict. How would you rate our recess experience on a scale from one to ten (one being full of conflict and ten being joyful for all)? Be ready to share.

Take some raised-hand shareouts about reasons for the ratings. Then use the content of the meeting to open a discussion about issues that might occur at recess. What issues might have risen among students during the ball toss greeting? During the activity? How might incorporating these games into incorporating these games into Morning Meeting proactively address some of the recess issues identified?

Open House—Open house and back-to-school events can begin with a Morning Meeting to set the tone and familiarize parents with the practice.

Example Open House Meeting

Good Evening to Anyone Who . . .
The leader says, "Good evening to anyone who . . ." and then finishes with categories like "has students in this school," "has more than one student in the school," "is new to this school," and so on. Individuals who fit these categories stand and greet each other.

Partner Sharing
Share with someone to your left or right, other than a family member, your response to the following: What is one thing you are looking forward to this school year?

Just Like Me
The leader stands in front of the group. Everyone else sits. The leader makes a positive statement such as "I like to read." Everyone to whom the statement applies stands up and says, "Just like me!" and then sits down again. The leader makes another statement and group members again respond. Continue through a number of statements.

Message to Parents
Post a message to parents at the beginning of the meeting:

Dear Parents,
We are excited to start this school year together with you and your children. Tonight we are going to discuss ways we can work collectively to make this the best year yet. As you are settling in, be thinking about one thing you are looking forward to this year. Be prepared to share.

Revisit the message to parents at the end of the meeting and share some ideas you heard.

Shaping School Culture

Morning Meeting is a powerful and proven tool for creating connection and cohesion in individual classrooms, and a schoolwide Morning Meeting can do the same for the larger community. Using the same four-part structure of greeting, sharing, activity, and message, students experience a familiar rhythm on a grander scale that connects them with all other classes in their school.

There's the added benefit of cultivating a schoolwide identity and positive spirit, as all students enjoy a shared experience. There are certainly considerations for facilitating a meeting with potentially hundreds of students and educators. But with careful planning, strategic implementation, and the teaching tool of interactive modeling, a schoolwide meeting can be a remarkable opportunity for schools and their communities.

Conclusion

The Power of Morning Meeting

"Morning Meeting is a silent bulldozer in the field of school reform," proclaimed Maurice Sykes many years ago when he was deputy superintendent for the District of Columbia school system. And it's true. When Morning Meeting is a regular part of a daily routine, it clears away the obstacles that impede children from feeling safe and engaged in school, creating the space for classroom members to take care of each other and to do their best learning. However, Morning Meetings do not just clear a space; they also help build what will fill that clearing.

Morning Meeting is not just a bulldozer but also a crane, hoisting and setting into place the blocks of a new and sturdy foundation: attentiveness, inquiry, kindness, respect, assertiveness, risk-taking, energy, and joy. Meeting after meeting, as members of the classroom community greet each other and share and play together, this foundation enables them to build a positive class-room, one within which students thrive.

With intangible constructions, unlike their counterparts of steel and concrete, it can be hard to measure the dimensions of our progress. It's slow, cumulative work, this building. But we listen and we watch and we see which blocks are solidly interlocked into place and which are shaky and need shoring up. And from time to time, when we get to step back and observe, we are heartened.

Day after day, in schools all over America, teachers who use the approach described in this book begin the day with meetings that are safe, challenging, and joyful circles of learning. Are there moments when the orderliness teeters and the teacher has to redirect students? Moments when someone forgets what respectful listening looks like and needs reminding? Of course, for that's what daily school life is like: vision and aspiration, steps forward and regular stumbles when students need a hand to regain their footing and move ahead again. Still, in every classroom that begins with Morning Meeting, students are engaged in learning and connecting with the people in the circle around them.

Morning Meeting is, on its surface, a simple and straightforward structure: everyone circled up beginning each day with four sequential components. The chapters in this book have described these components and the many ways in which they build social and academic skills, as well as classroom community. All the skills that it teaches are essential to help children grow and develop into smart, principled, and caring adults. However, with Morning Meeting, as with many simple and straightforward designs, the impact of the whole is greater than the sum of its parts and results in more than the acquisition of specific skills.

There is a pervasive sense of urgency in our country about whether students will be well prepared for high school, college, and the future they will face. And, as always, there are advocates for simply accelerating the pace of instruction, crowding more and more into the days of elementary school children—and their teachers. Fortunately, there are also strong and respected voices reminding us how critical it is to foster deeper attributes that promote and sustain success: curiosity, persistence, and empathy, to name a few. These are some of the very attributes that Morning Meeting nurtures, and time used for them does not distract from, but rather fortifies, achievement. As one teacher said of Morning Meeting, "Those tools, the simple strategies and clear structures, move us in the direction of profound goals. Sometimes we don't even know the full import of what's happening for a long time."

What we do know is this: In the safe learning communities that Morning Meeting helps build, students speak and listen to each other, they play and work together—day after day, year after year. Along with academic strengths, they develop a sense of who they are and what is of value. And they develop strong and respectful voices along with the skills to deploy those voices toward varied and positive ends: to inquire, to explain, to console, to assert, to stand up for a friend or a conviction. Wherever students journey and whatever joys and challenges their journeys bring, these abilities will serve them and the world they inhabit.

References

Bellanca, James, and Ron Brandt, eds. 2010. *21st Century Skills: Rethinking How Students Learn*. Bloomington, IN: Solution Tree.

Blum, Robert W. 2005. "A Case for School Connectedness." *Educational Leadership* 62 no. 7 (April): 16–20. http://www.ascd.org/publications/educational-leadership/apr05/vol62/num07/A-Case-for-School-Connectedness.aspx.

Common Core State Standards Initiative. 2010. "Common Core State Standards for English Language Arts and Literacy in History/Social Studies, Science, and Technical Subjects." http://www.corestandards.org/wp-content/uploads/ELA_Standards1.pdf.

Durlak, Joseph A., Roger P. Weissberg, Allison B. Dymnicki, Rebecca D. Taylor, and Kriston B. Schellinger. 2011. "The Impact of Enhancing Students' Social and Emotional Learning: A Meta-Analysis of School-Based Universal Interventions." *Child Development* 82, no. 1: 405–432. https://doi.org/10.1111/j.1467-8624.2010.01564.x.

Elias, Maurice J., Joseph E. Zins, Roger P. Weissberg, Karin S. Frey, Mark T. Greenberg, Norris M. Haynes, Rachael Kessler, Mary E. Schwab-Stone, and Timothy P. Shriver. 1997. *Promoting Social and Emotional Learning: Guidelines for Educators*. Alexandria, VA: Association for Supervision and Curriculum Development.

Goodson, Barbara, and Carolyn Layzer. 2009. *Learning to Talk and Listen: An Oral Language Resource for Early Childhood Caregivers*. Washington, DC: National Institute for Literacy.

O'Kearney, Richard, Karen Salmon, Maria Liwag, Clare-Ann Fortune, and Amy Dawel. 2017. "Emotional Abilities in Children With Oppositional Defiant Disorder (ODD): Impairments in Perspective-Taking and Understanding Mixed Emotions Are Associated With High Callous-Unemotional Traits." *Child Psychiatry and Human Development* 48, no. 2, 346–357. https://doi.org/10.1007/s10578-016-0645-4.

Palmer, Parker J. 2007. *The Courage to Teach: Exploring the Inner Landscape of a Teacher's Life*. San Francisco: Jossey-Bass.

Renner, Ben. 2018. "American Families Spend Just 37 Minutes of Quality Time Together per Day, Survey Finds." Study Finds. March 21, 2018. https://studyfinds.org/american-families-spend-37-minutes-quality-time/.

Renner, Ben. 2020. "Modern Family: Average Parent Spends Just 5 Hours Face-to-Face With Their Kids per Week!" Study Finds. January 25, 2020. https://studyfinds.org/modern-family-average-parent-spends-just-5-hours-face-to-face-with-their-kids-per-week/.

Rideout, Victoria J., Ulla G. Foehr, and Donald F. Roberts. 2010. *Generation M^2: Media in the Lives of 8-to 18-Year-Olds*. Menlo Park, CA: Kaiser Family Foundation.

Rogoff, Barbara. 1990. *Apprenticeship in Thinking: Cognitive Development in Social Context*. San Francisco: Oxford University Press.

Susic, Peter. "18+ Teen & Kids Screen Time Statistics (2023): Avg. Screen Time for Teens." Headphones Addict. February 21, 2023. https://headphonesaddict.com/teen-kids-screen-time-statistics/.

Talking in Class. 2015. "Talking to Learn: Harnessing the Power of Student Conversation." Edutopia. February 13, 2015. https://www.edutopia.org/discussion/talking-learn-harnessing-power-student-conversation.

Varsity Brands. 2014. "School Spirit: The Connection Between Student Achievement, Involvement, and Confidence." Working paper, The Harris Poll. https://files.varsity.com/publications/varsity-brands-white-paper.html.

Zwiers, Jeff, and Marie Crawford. 2011. *Academic Conversations: Classroom Talk That Fosters Critical Thinking and Content Understandings*. Portland, ME: Stenhouse.

Further Resources

All of the recommended practices in this book come from or are consistent with the *Responsive Classroom* approach to teaching—an evidence-based education approach associated with greater teacher effectiveness, higher student achievement, and improved school climate. *Responsive Classroom* practices help educators build competencies in four interrelated domains: engaging academics, positive community, effective management, and developmentally responsive teaching. To learn more, see the following resources published by Center for Responsive Schools and available at www.responsiveclassroom.org.

Effective Management: Set up and run a classroom in ways that enable the best possible teaching and learning.

Interactive Modeling: A Powerful Technique for Teaching Children by Margaret Berry Wilson. 2012.

What Every Teacher Needs to Know, K-5 series, by Margaret Berry Wilson and Mike Anderson. 2010-2011.

Empowering Educators: A Comprehensive Guide to Teaching Grades K, 1, 2 by Kirsten Lee Howard, Amy Wade, Becky Wanless, and Lisa Dewey Wells. 2021.

Empowering Educators: A Comprehensive Guide to Teaching Grades 3, 4, 5 by Julie Kelly, Andy Moral, Jenni Lee Groegler Pierson, and Amanda Stessen-Blevins. 2021.

Empowering Educators: A Comprehensive Guide to Teaching Grades 6, 7, 8 by Linda Berger, Emily Parrelli, Brian Smith, and Heather Young. 2021.

Teaching Children to Care: Classroom Management for Ethical and Academic Growth K–8, revised ed., by Ruth Sidney Charney. 2002.

Morning Meeting: Gather as a whole class each morning to greet each other, share news, and warm up for the day of learning ahead.

80 Morning Meeting Ideas for Grades K–2 by Susan Lattanzi Roser. 2012.

80 Morning Meeting Ideas for Grades 3–6 by Carol Davis. 2012.

Doing Math in Morning Meeting: 150 Quick Activities That Connect to Your Curriculum by Andy Dousis and Margaret Berry Wilson. 2010. (Includes a Common Core State Standards correlation guide.)

Doing Science in Morning Meeting: 150 Quick Activities That Connect to Your Curriculum by Lara Webb and Margaret Berry Wilson. 2013. (Includes correlation guides to the Next Generation Science Standards and A Framework for K–12 Science Education, the basis for the standards.)

Doing Language Arts in Morning Meeting: 150 Quick Activities That Connect to Your Curriculum by Jodie Luongo, Joan Riordan, and Kate Umstatter. 2015. (Includes a Common Core State Standards correlation guide.)

Doing Social Studies in Morning Meeting: 150 Quick Activities That Connect to Your Curriculum by Leah Carson and Jane Cofie. 2017. (Includes correlation guides to the National Curriculum Standards for Social Studies—The Themes of Social Studies, the College, Career, & Civic Life C3 Framework for Social Studies State Standards, and the Common Core State Standards for English Language Arts.)

Positive Teacher Language: Use words and tone as a tool to promote students' active learning, sense of community, and self-discipline.

The Power of Our Words: Teacher Language That Helps Children Learn, 2nd ed., by Paula Denton, EdD. 2014.

Engaging Academics: Learn tools for effective teaching and making lessons lively, appropriately challenging, and purposeful to help students develop higher levels of motivation, persistence, and mastery of skills and content.

The Joyful Classroom: Practical Ways to Engage and Challenge Elementary Students. From *Responsive Classroom* with Lynn Bechtel and Kristen Vincent. 2016.

Make Learning Meaningful: How to Leverage the Brain's Natural Learning Cycle in K–8 Classrooms by Kristen Vincent. 2021.

The Language of Learning: Teaching Students Core Thinking, Speaking, and Listening Skills by Margaret Berry Wilson. 2014.

Teaching Discipline: Use practical proactive and reactive strategies such as rule creation, Interactive Modeling, and logical consequences to promote self-discipline in students and build a safe, calm, and respectful school climate.

Teaching Self-Discipline: The Responsive Classroom Guide to Helping Students Dream, Behave, and Achieve in Elementary School. From *Responsive Classroom* with Laurie Badge, Suzy Ghosh, Earl Hunter II, Caitie Meehan, and Cory Wade. 2018.

Teasing, Tattling, Defiance and More: Positive Approaches to 10 Common Classroom Behaviors by Margaret Berry Wilson. 2013.

Responsive School Discipline: Essentials for Elementary School Leaders by Chip Wood and Babs Freeman-Loftis. 2011.

Foundation-Setting During the First Weeks of School: Take time in the critical first weeks of school to establish expectations, routines, a sense of community, and a positive classroom tone.

The First Six Weeks of School, 2nd ed. From *Responsive Classroom*. 2015.

Movement, Games, Songs, and Chants: Sprinkle quick, lively activities throughout the school day to keep students energized, engaged, and alert.

Closing Circles: 50 Activities for Ending the Day in a Positive Way by Dana Januszka and Kristen Vincent. 2012.

Energizers! 88 Quick Movement Activities That Refresh and Refocus by Susan Lattanzi Roser. 2009.

50 More Energizers! Purposeful Play That Leads to Learning by Melissa Shoup Gheen. 2022.

99 Activities and Greetings: Great for Morning Meeting . . . and Other Meetings, Too! by Melissa Correa-Connolly. 2004.

Preventing Bullying at School: Use practical strategies throughout the day to create a safe, kind environment in which bullying is far less likely to take root.

How to Bullyproof Your Classroom, 2nd ed., by Caltha Crowe. 2021. (Includes bullying prevention lessons.)

Solving Behavior Problems With Children: Engage students in solving their behavior problems so they feel safe, challenged, and invested in changing.

Sammy and His Behavior Problems: Stories and Strategies from a Teacher's Year by Caltha Crowe. 2010.

Solving Thorny Behavior Problems: How Teachers and Students Can Work Together by Caltha Crowe. 2009.

Child Development: Understand children's common physical, social-emotional, cognitive, and language characteristics at each age, and adapt teaching to respond to children's developmental needs.

Yardsticks: Child and Adolescent Development Ages 4–14, 4th ed., by Chip Wood. 2017.

Yardsticks Guide Series: Common Developmental Characteristics in the Classroom and at Home, Grades K–8 (based on *Yardsticks* by Chip Wood). From *Responsive Classroom*. 2018.

Special Area Educators: Explore key *Responsive Classroom* practices adapted for a wide variety of special areas.

Responsive Classroom for Music, Art, PE, and Other Special Areas. From *Responsive Classroom*. 2016.

Professional Development/Staff Meetings: Learn easy-to-use structures for getting the most out of your work with colleagues.

Energize Your Meetings! 35 Interactive Learning Structures for Educators. From *Responsive Classroom*. 2014.

About the Author

As the author of the fourth edition, Karen Poplawski brings decades of experience from her time spent in schools and working alongside educators to implement the *Responsive Classroom* approach. Karen serves as the chief programs officer for *Responsive Classroom* at Center for Responsive Schools and for more than ten years has led the development and refinement of Morning Meeting and other *Responsive Classroom* practices to ensure that this powerful approach continues to influence the lives of students and educators.

Photo by Kelsey Kalene Photography

Acknowledgments

We would like to thank Jane Cofie, the director for curriculum and instructional design for *Responsive Classroom*, for organizing and curating video to enhance this edition of *The Morning Meeting Book*. We would also like to thank the following teachers, students, and schools for opening their classroom doors and sharing their Morning Meeting experience with us:

- Eliza Baker Magnet School, Minneapolis, MN: Julia Monke and her first grade students

- Greenbriar East Elementary, Chantilly, VA: Michelle Minor and her fourth grade students

- Missoula International School, Missoula, MT: Patricia Cano and her second/third grade students

We would also like to acknowledge and thank Carmela Pine for providing new tried and tested greeting, sharing, group activity, and message ideas to enhance the content of this book.

Finally, we would like to acknowledge and thank educators everywhere who take time out of their day to bring the joy of Morning Meeting to their classroom and school spaces. The world is a better place with you teaching in it.

About the Publisher

Center for Responsive Schools, Inc., a not-for-profit educational organization, offers professional development, curriculum, and books and resources to support academic, social, and emotional learning.

Center for Responsive Schools (CRS) is the developer of *Responsive Classroom*®, a research-based education approach associated with greater teacher effectiveness, higher student achievement, and improved school climate, and of Fly Five, a comprehensive social-emotional learning curriculum for kindergarten through eighth grade.

Center for Responsive Schools' vision is to influence and inspire a world-class education for every student in every school, every day, and to bring hope and joy to educators and students alike. Visit us at crslearn.org to learn more:

Index